Not Just Cheesecake!

Not Just Cheesecake!

The Low-Fat, Low-Cholesterol, Low-Calorie
Great Dessert Cookbook

Marilyn Stone
Shelley Melvin
Charlie Crawford

Foreword by Gail Kauwell, M.Ag., R.D.

TRIAD PUBLISHING COMPANY   GAINESVILLE, FLORIDA

Printed in the United States of America

Library of Congress Cataloging-in-Publication Data
Stone, Marilyn.
  Not Just Cheesecake!

  Includes index.
    1. Low-fat diet--Recipes.   2. Desserts.   3. Yogurt cheese.
4. Cookery (Yogurt).   I. Melvin, Shelley, 1944-
II. Crawford, Charlie.   III. Title.
RM237.7.S86   1988   641.8'6   88-11648
ISBN 0-937404-29-2 (pbk.)

Nutrition information for yogurt cheese is based on independent laboratory analyses of yogurt cheese made with Dannon non-fat and Dannon lowfat vanilla yogurt, drained in the Really Creamy yogurt cheese funnel. All figures are approximate and may vary, as the nutritional content of yogurt varies from one carton to another. Figures may also vary with brand of yogurt and draining time.

Published and distribtuted by Triad Publishing Co., Inc., 1110 NW Eighth Ave. Gainesville, FL 32601. For information on bulk orders write Special Sales Dept.

Cover photo: John Moran

Marilyn Stone has worked as a cookbook editor in the publishing industry. She is the author/editor of *The Chosen: Appetizers and Desserts.*

Shelley Melvin is a cooking instructor, caterer, and former consumer advisor for a leading food processor manufacturer. She is the author/editor of *Quick & Easy.*

Charlie Crawford is owner of The White Apron, a catering company specializing in fabulous desserts. He does freelance foodstyling and menu consultation for restaurants.

Gail Kauwell, M.Ag., R.D., is an assistant professor in the Clinical and Community Dietetics Program at the University of Florida. She is the recipient of the 1988 Distinguished Dietitian of Florida award.

Contents

Foreword

Reducing the amount of fat in your diet is probably one of the most important steps you can take toward developing a healthy eating style. But if you're like most Americans, the idea of giving up or decreasing your intake of high fat foods, especially rich desserts, can seem difficult or unappealing.

The truth is, you don't have to sacrifice good taste or desserts to achieve this dietary modification. In fact, you won't believe your tastebuds when you sample the recipes in this cookbook. What's even more incredible is the nutritional value of the recipes. Imagine, great tasting desserts that contain up to half the calories, fat and sodium of traditional desserts! Add the fact that these desserts are higher in calcium than most desserts, and you've got a real bonus.

How can this be? Well, it's easy, thanks to a delicious substitute for cream cheese. It's called yogurt cheese. Desserts with yogurt cheese are a cinch to make and are proof that good tasting foods don't have to be high in calories, fat, and sodium.

So go ahead, put dessert back into your diet and enjoy the sensory delights of rich tasting and nutritious creamy yogurt cheese desserts, without the guilt.

GAIL KAUWELL, M.Ag., R.D.

Introduction

Yogurt cheese has been around for a long time. In fact, *laban* (the Arabic name for yogurt cheese) has been a part of Middle Eastern cuisines for centuries. *Jane Brody's Good Food Book, The Frugal Gourmet,* and many other well known cookbooks include recipes using it. Still, the general public remains largely unaware of its existence.

This is a good time for Americans to get acquainted with yogurt cheese and start reaping the benefits. Most of us need to lose weight, to cut our intake of fat and cholesterol, to lower sodium intake, yet we are hard-pressed to stay on our diets because, as everyone knows, reducing diets are unsatisfying, low-fat and low-cholesterol diets restrict cheese and other rich foods, and low-sodium diets can be tasteless.

Yogurt cheese to the rescue!

According to the University of California, Berkeley *Wellness Letter,* "yogurt cheese can be an excellent substitute for high-fat cheeses, sandwich spreads, and dips. What makes yogurt cheese special is that it picks up the flavor of anything it's mixed with."

Cardiac Alert, a newsletter dedicated to prevention of heart disease, states, "Because yogurt cheese is low in sodium and low in fat, it is a healthy addition to anyone's diet. It is especially useful, however, for people with high blood pressure and heart disease."

Gaylord Hauser, the guru of health and nutrition in

the 40s and 50s, called yogurt cheese "the tenderest, creamiest cream cheese you ever ate; protein-rich, calcium and vitamin B-rich, but not fat!"

What more could anyone ask of a food?

About Yogurt Cheese

As you get acquainted with yogurt cheese, you'll soon discover its wonderful versatility. It is the perfect substitute for cream cheese and other soft cheeses, sour cream, and even mayonnaise because, not only is it much lower in fat and calories, it takes on any flavor it is mixed with. Its own flavor is part way between cream cheese and sour cream.

HOW TO MAKE YOGURT CHEESE

Place yogurt into a draining device and allow to drain 2 to 24 hours, until cheese is the desired consistency. (Approximately half the yogurt will become cheese and half will become whey.) Discard whey. Keep cheese in the refrigerator in a covered container. Whey may continue releasing, so pour off any accumulated liquid before using.

TYPES OF DRAINING DEVICES

The "traditional" method of making the cheese was to spoon yogurt into cheesecloth, tie it into a bag, and let it drain overnight suspended over the kitchen sink. Most people today find this too messy and awkward to bother with. If you want to have yogurt cheese as a dietary staple, readily available for any and all purposes, you will want to use a more convenient method. The easiest way to make the cheese is with a specially designed yogurt cheesemaker, such as the yogurt cheese funnel.

LENGTH OF TIME TO MAKE CHEESE

Even though most of the recipes suggest draining the yogurt "the day before," there is a wide, normal variation in how yogurt drains. Once you get used to your favorite yogurt, you will know how to plan. In 2 hours the amount of whey (from 16 ounces of yogurt) can range from 2.5 ounces to 6 ounces; it takes at least 8 or 9 hours to produce a very dry cream cheese, and some yogurts may require a draining time of 24 hours.

WHAT KIND OF YOGURT TO USE

Use any natural yogurt, either plain or flavored (vanilla, lemon, coffee) that does not contain gelatin. Gelatin holds the whey in the yogurt and does not allow it to drain off.

Sometimes you will find a carton of yogurt without gelatin or stabilizers that does not release its whey. This may be due to the processing temperature. Try a carton from another batch or different processing plant (that information is on the label), or use another brand of yogurt for a while.

COOKING WITH YOGURT CHEESE

Cold yogurt cheese mixes easily with a fork or wire whisk. Vigorous mixing or beating (whether by hand or with an electric mixer, blender or food processor) is not necessary and not recommended. Always treat the cheese gently.

Like all milk products, yogurt cheese is sensitive to heat. Do not heat for a long time or allow to boil. You can prevent separation or thinning of the cheese during cooking by combining it with flour, cornstarch, or eggs.

Cool hot foods before mixing with yogurt cheese. Another option is to stir a small amount of the hot food into the cheese to warm it, then slowly add the cheese to the hot food, stirring constantly. When possible, add yogurt cheese to hot foods at the end of the cooking time.

14

Ingredients and Equipment

EQUIPMENT AND PROCEDURES

BAKING PANS

Cheesecakes baked in a pie pan are flatter than those made in a springform, and therefore take less baking time. When a 7-inch springform pan is used, baking times are longer but the cake is higher and servings look much bigger! (7-inch springforms are available at kitchenware shops, or see ordering information.)

YOGURT CHEESE DRAINING DEVICES

This equipment is available in kitchenware shops and health food stores. Since this is a fairly new type of product, you may not find yogurt cheesemaking equipment in your area. Ordering information is included at the back of the book.

MICROWAVE COOKING

Baking instructions are given for a conventional oven. A microwave can be used for cheesecake or cheese pie recipes. Spoon mixture into an 8-inch microwave-safe round baking dish. Microwave for 12 minutes on high power, turning one-quarter turn every 3 minutes. Refrigerate 24 hours before serving.

GREASING PANS

When a lightly greased pan is called for, a non-stick vegetable spray may used instead.

FREEZING

Cheesecakes made with yogurt cheese freeze well, just as any cheesecake. Yogurt cheese may also be frozen; afterwards the texture is grainy but that disappears with mixing.

INGREDIENTS

EGGS AND SUBSTITUTIONS

Some of the baked cheesecakes use whole eggs, which yield a slightly more creamy product. In any of these, you can reduce fat, cholesterol, and calories by substituting —for 2 whole eggs—1 whole egg and 2 whites, 3 egg whites, or a cholesterol-free product such as Egg Beaters or Scramblers. (Refer to package for instructions and nutrition information. Omit cornstarch in the recipe if the egg replacement is a starch product, such as Egg Replacer.) When you use the nutritional data table (page 18) for new values, keep in mind that any change must be divided by the number of servings.

YOGURT/YOGURT CHEESE

Yogurt for making yogurt cheese must be natural and free from gelatin.

Recipe quantities are given for the yogurt, not the yogurt cheese. You do not have to measure the resulting cheese because exact amounts are not critical.

Recipes using lowfat vanilla yogurt can be adapted to nonfat plain yogurt by adding sugar and vanilla to taste.

PIE CRUST

A crust can add fat and calories to a pie or cheese-cake, and most of the time it isn't really necessary to have a crust to satisfy your need for a "real" dessert. Therefore, most of the recipes in this book omit the crust. We have included a few moderately low-fat crust recipes for those occasions when you have company coming or just want to splurge.

SWEETENERS

Fruit juice concentrate, fruit spread, honey, or grain sweetener may be used in place of sugar according to taste. In some recipes we have used all-fruit jams (conserves) that have no added sugar but are sweetened with fruit juices, giving them good, rich fruit flavors.

You may prefer to substitute an artificial sweetener for the sugar. Before baking, make sure the sweetener you are using may be cooked.

NUTRITIONAL INFORMATION

The nutritional information for each recipe is based on the first ingredient given (where there are options) and any ingredient labeled "optional" has not been counted. Use the table on the following page for calculating new values when you make substitutions.

Exchanges: According to exchanges based on 1986 revision of *Exchange Lists for Meal Planning* developed by the American Diabetes Association and the American Dietetic Association, one serving of Easy Cheesecake (page 21) can be substituted for one serving of lowfat milk. Consult your physician if you are on a medically restricted diet.

NUTRITIONAL DATA FOR INGREDIENTS

FOOD	CALORIES	FAT (gm)	CHOLESTEROL (mg)	SODIUM (mg)	CARBO-HYDRATES (gm)	CALCIUM (mg)	PROTEIN (gm)
Cornstarch, 1 Tbsp	63	trace	0	trace	7	0	trace
Egg, 1 large	79	6	274	69	1	28	6
Egg white, 1 large	16	0	0	55	1	3	3
Egg yolk, 1 large	63	6	274	14	0	25	3
Graham cracker, 1 whole	54	1	n/a	94	10	5	1
Sugar, 1 Tbsp white, granulated	48	0	0	0	12	0	0
Yogurt cheese, 1 cup from nonfat	160	0	0	160	17	560	18
Yogurt cheese, 1 cup from plain lowfat	200	6	*11	144	10	*480	22
Yogurt cheese, 1 cup from vanilla lowfat	248	7	*11	160	26	480	18
Zwieback toast, 1 pc	30	1	n/a	16	5	1	1

* approximate

The nutritional information is this book is based on yogurt cheese made from *Dannon* vanilla and non-fat yogurt, drained in the *Really Creamy* Yogurt Cheese Funnel.

Chapter 1

Really Creamy
Cheesecakes

Easy Cheesecake

32-ounce carton vanilla-flavored lowfat yogurt
2 tablespoons sugar (or more to taste)
1 tablespoon cornstarch
1 tablespoon lemon juice (optional)
1 teaspoon vanilla
2 eggs, lightly beaten (for substitutes, see page 16)

Day before: Drain yogurt to make yogurt cheese (see p. 13).

1. Preheat oven to 325 degrees. Lightly grease an 8-inch pie pan or 7-inch springform pan.

2. Place yogurt cheese in a medium-size bowl. Add sugar, cornstarch, lemon juice, and vanilla, mixing gently with a fork or wire whisk until well blended. Stir in the eggs.

3. Pour into the prepared pan and smooth the top with a spatula. Bake until center is set: 20 to 25 minutes for a pie pan, or 45 to 55 minutes for a springform.

4. Cool slightly on a wire rack. Refrigerate until chilled.

    Serves 8.

Per serving: Calories 99; Protein 6 gm; Carbohydrates 11 gm; Fat 3 gm; Cholesterol 71 mg; Calcium 127 mg; Sodium 57 mg

Apple Bavarian Cheesecake

32-ounce carton vanilla-flavored lowfat yogurt
1 tablespoon cornstarch
2 eggs, lightly beaten (for substitutes, see page 16)
1 large apple, peeled and thinly sliced
2 tablespoons sugar
$1/2$ teaspoon cinnamon

Day before: Drain yogurt to make yogurt cheese (see p. 13).

1. Preheat oven to 325 degrees. Lightly grease a 7-inch springform pan.

2. Place yogurt cheese in a medium-size bowl. Add the cornstarch, stirring gently with a fork or wire whisk until well blended. Stir in the eggs.

3. Combine sliced apple, sugar and cinnamon in a separate bowl. Set aside.

4. Pour cheesecake mixture into the prepared pan and smooth the top with a spatula. Spread with apple topping. Bake for 55 minutes.

5. Cool slightly on a wire rack. Refrigerate until chilled.

    Serves 8.

Per serving: Calories 113; Protein 6 gm; Carbohydrates 15 gm; Fat 3 gm; Cholesterol 71 mg; Calcium 130 mg; Sodium 57 mg

Apple Butter Cheesecake

32-ounce carton vanilla-flavored lowfat yogurt
1/4 cup sugar
2 tablespoons cornstarch
1/2 cup unsweetened apple butter
2 tablespoons apple brandy (optional)
2 eggs, lightly beaten (for substitutes, see page 16)

Day before: Drain yogurt to make yogurt cheese (see p. 13).

1. Preheat oven to 325 degrees. Lightly grease an 8-inch pie pan or 7-inch springform pan.

2. Place yogurt cheese in a medium-size bowl. Add the sugar, cornstarch, apple butter, and brandy, mixing gently with a fork or wire whisk until well blended. Stir in the eggs.

3. Pour into the prepared pan and smooth the top with a spatula. Bake until center is set: 20 to 25 minutes for a pie pan, or 45 to 55 minutes for a springform.

4. Cool slightly on a wire rack. Refrigerate until chilled.

Serves 8.

Per serving: Calories 142; Protein 6 gm; Carbohydrates 22 gm; Fat 3 gm; Cholesterol 71 mg; Calcium 132 mg; Sodium 91 mg

Apricot Cheesecake

32-ounce carton vanilla-flavored yogurt
2 tablespoons cornstarch
$1/4$ cup apricot preserves
1 teaspoon vanilla extract
1 egg, lightly beaten (for substitutes, see page 16)
2 egg whites, lightly beaten

Day before: Drain yogurt to make yogurt cheese (see p. 13).

1. Preheat oven to 325 degrees. Lightly grease an 8-inch pie pan or 7-inch springform pan.

2. Place yogurt cheese in a medium-size bowl. Add the cornstarch, apricot preserves, and vanilla extract, mixing gently with a fork or wire whisk until well blended. Stir in the eggs.

3. Pour into the prepared pan and smooth the top with a spatula. Bake until center is set: 20 to 25 minutes for a pie pan, or 45 to 55 minutes for a springform.

4. Cool slightly on a wire rack. Refrigerate until chilled.

Serves 8.

Per serving: Calories 112; Protein 6 gm; Carbohydrates 16 gm; Fat 2 gm; Cholesterol 37 mg; Calcium 126 mg; Sodium 62 mg

Banana Cheesecake

32-ounce carton vanilla-flavored yogurt
2 medium-size overripe bananas (about 1 cup)
2 tablespoons strawberry fruit spread
2 tablespoons cornstarch
2 eggs, lightly beaten (for substitutes, see page 16)
Sugar to taste, optional

Day before: Drain yogurt to make yogurt cheese (see p. 13).

1. Preheat oven to 325 degrees. Lightly grease an 8-inch pie pan or 7-inch springform pan.

2. In a medium bowl, mash the bananas with a fork until smooth. Add the yogurt cheese, cornstarch and strawberry spread, mixing gently with a fork or wire whisk until well blended. Stir in the eggs.

3. Pour into the prepared pan and smooth the top with a spatula. Bake until center is set: 25 minutes for a pie pan, or 55 minutes for a springform.

4. Cool slightly on a wire rack. Refrigerate for 24 hours. (The flavors improve the second day.)

Serves 8.

Per serving: Calories 134; Protein 6 gm; Carbohydrates 20 gm; Fat 3 gm; Cholesterol 71 mg; Calcium 129 mg; Sodium 58 mg

Cherry Almond Cheesecake

32-ounce carton vanilla-flavored lowfat yogurt
1 can (16 oz) water-packed tart red cherries
$1/4$ cup sugar (or to taste)
2 tablespoons cornstarch
$1/4$ teaspoon almond extract
2 eggs, lightly beaten (for substitutes, see page 16)

Day before: Drain yogurt to make yogurt cheese (see p. 13).

Day before: Drain yogurt to make yogurt cheese (see p. 13).

1. Preheat oven to 325 degrees. Lightly grease an 8-inch pie pan or 7-inch springform pan.

2. Drain cherries, reserving liquid for glaze if desired (see recipe). Sprinkle sugar over cherries and stir.

3. Place yogurt cheese in a medium-size bowl. Add cherries, cornstarch, and almond extract, mixing gently with a fork or wire whisk until well blended. Stir in eggs.

4. Pour into the prepared pan and smooth the top with a spatula. Bake until center is set: 20 to 25 minutes for a pie pan, or 45 to 55 minutes for a springform.

5. Cool slightly on a wire rack. Refrigerate until chilled.

    Serves 8.

Per serving: Calories 136; Protein 6 gm; Carbohydrates 21 gm; Fat 3 gm; Cholesterol 71 mg; Calcium 136 mg; Sodium 58 mg

Cranberry-Orange Cheesecake

32-ounce carton vanilla-flavored lowfat yogurt
2 tablespoons cornstarch
$^1/_2$ cup whole berry cranberry sauce
1 teaspoon grated orange peel (or more to taste)
1 tablespoon orange liqueur (optional)
2 eggs, lightly beaten (for substitutes, see page 16)

Day before: Drain yogurt to make yogurt cheese (see p. 13).

1. Preheat oven to 325 degrees. Lightly grease an 8-inch pie pan or 7-inch springform pan.

2. Place yogurt cheese in a medium-size bowl. Add cornstarch, cranberry sauce, orange peel, and liqueur, stirring gently with a fork or wire whisk until well blended. Stir in the eggs.

3. Pour into the prepared pan and smooth the top with a spatula. Bake until center is set: 25 to 30 minutes for a pie pan, or 55 to 60 minutes for a springform.

4. Cool slightly on a wire rack. Refrigerate until chilled.

Serves 8.

Per serving: Calories 114; Protein 6 gm; Carbohydrates 15 gm; Fat 3 gm; Cholesterol 71 mg; Calcium 128 mg; Sodium 57 mg

Key Lime Cheesecake

32-ounce carton vanilla-flavored lowfat yogurt
$1/4$ cup sugar
2 tablespoons cornstarch
2 tablespoons key lime juice
2 eggs, lightly beaten (for substitutes, see page 16)

Day before: Drain yogurt to make yogurt cheese (see p. 13).

1. Preheat oven to 325 degrees. Lightly grease an 8-inch pie pan or 7-inch springform pan.

2. Place yogurt cheese in a medium-size bowl. Add sugar, cornstarch, and lime juice, mixing gently with a fork or wire whisk until well blended. Stir in the eggs.

3. Pour into the prepared pan and smooth the top with a spatula. Bake until center is set: 25 to 30 minutes for a pie pan, or 55 to 60 minutes for a springform.

4. Cool slightly on a wire rack. Refrigerate until chilled.

    Serves 8.

Per serving: Calories 114; Protein 6 gm; Carbohydrates 15 gm; Fat 3 gm; Cholesterol 71 mg; Calcium 127 mg; Sodium 58 mg

Orange Cheesecake I

32-ounce carton vanilla-flavored lowfat yogurt
2 tablespoons cornstarch
$1/4$ cup orange marmalade
1 tablespoon orange liqueur
$1/4$ teaspoon orange flavoring (optional)
2 eggs, lightly beaten (for substitutes, see page 16)

Day before: Drain yogurt to make yogurt cheese (see p. 13).

1.   Preheat oven to 325 degrees. Lightly grease an 8-inch pie pan or 7-inch springform pan.

2.   Place yogurt cheese in a medium-size bowl. Add cornstarch, marmalade, liqueur, and flavoring, stirring gently with a fork or wire whisk until well blended. Stir in the eggs.

3.   Pour into the prepared pan and smooth the top with a spatula. Bake until center is set: 25 to 30 minutes for a pie pan, or 55 to 60 minutes for a springform.

4.   Cool slightly on a wire rack. Refrigerate until chilled.

Serves 8.

Per serving: Calories 120; Protein 6 gm; Carbohydrates 15 gm; Fat 3 gm; Cholesterol 71 mg; Calcium 130 mg; Sodium 59 mg

Orange Cheesecake II

32-ounce carton vanilla-flavored lowfat yogurt
2 tablespoons sugar (or to taste)
1 teaspoon grated orange peel
1 tablespoon cornstarch
2 eggs, lightly beaten (for substitutes, see page 16)

Topping
1 cup orange juice
1 tablespoon sugar (optional)
2 tablespoons cornstarch
1 orange, peeled and sectioned

Day before: Drain yogurt to make yogurt cheese (see p. 13).

1. Preheat oven to 325 degrees. Lightly grease a 7-inch springform pan.

2. Place yogurt cheese in a medium-size bowl. Add the sugar, cornstarch and grated orange peel, mixing gently with a fork or whisk until well blended. Stir in the eggs.

3. Pour into the prepared pan and smooth the top with a spatula. Bake until center is set, 45 to 55 minutes.

4. Cool slightly on a wire rack. Refrigerate until chilled.

5. Topping: Mix cornstarch with a small amount of juice. Add remaining juice and stir over medium heat until thickened. Cool slightly. Spread half over cake and decorate with orange sections dipped in remaining mixture.

Serves 8.

Per serving: Calories 127; Protein 6 gm; Carbohydrates 18 gm; Fat 3 gm; Cholesterol 71 mg; Calcium 137 mg; Sodium 57 mg

Pineapple Cheesecake

32-ounce carton vanilla-flavored lowfat yogurt
$\frac{1}{4}$ cup sugar
2 tablespoons cornstarch
1 tablespoon rum (optional)
$\frac{1}{2}$ teaspoon pineapple flavoring (optional)
1 can (20 oz) crushed pineapple, packed in own juice
2 eggs, lightly beaten (for substitutes, see page 16)

Day before: Drain yogurt to make yogurt cheese (see p. 13).

1. Preheat oven to 325 degrees. Lightly grease an 8-inch pie pan or 7-inch springform pan. Drain pineapple in a sieve, pressing with a spoon to remove as much liquid as possible.

2. Place yogurt cheese in a medium-size bowl. Add sugar, cornstarch, flavorings, and pineapple, stirring gently with a fork until well blended. Stir in the eggs.

3. Pour into the prepared pan and smooth the top with a spatula. Bake until center is set: 25 to 30 minutes for a pie pan, or 55 to 60 minutes for a springform.

4. Cool slightly on a wire rack. Refrigerate until chilled.

    Serves 8.

Per serving: Calories 146; Protein 6 gm; Carbohydrates 22 gm; Fat 3 gm; Cholesterol 71 mg; Calcium 135 mg; Sodium 58 mg

Pina Colada Cheesecake

32-ounce carton vanilla-flavored lowfat yogurt
$\frac{1}{4}$ cup sugar
2 tablespoons cornstarch
1 tablespoon cream of coconut (non-alcoholic drink mix)
1 can (20 oz) crushed pineapple, packed in own juice
1 teaspoon rum extract
$\frac{1}{2}$ teaspoon coconut flavoring (optional)
2 eggs, lightly beaten (for substitutes, see page 16)

Day before: Drain yogurt to make yogurt cheese (see p. 13).

1. Preheat oven to 325 degrees. Lightly grease an 8-inch pie pan or 7-inch springform pan. Drain pineapple in a sieve, pressing with a spoon to remove as much liquid as possible.

2. Place yogurt cheese in a medium-size bowl. Add sugar, cornstarch, cream of coconut, flavorings and pineapple, mixing gently with a fork or wire whisk until well blended. Stir in the eggs.

3. Pour into the prepared pan and smooth the top with a spatula. Bake until center is set: 25 to 30 minutes for a pie pan, or 55 to 60 minutes for a springform.

4. Cool slightly on a wire rack. Refrigerate until chilled.

    Serves 8.

    Per serving: Calories 164; Protein 6 gm; Carbohydrates 26 gm; Fat 4 gm; Cholesterol 71 mg; Calcium 137 mg; Sodium 59 mg

Raspberry Swirl Cheesecake

32-ounce carton vanilla-flavored lowfat yogurt
1 tablespoon cornstarch
$\frac{1}{2}$ teaspoon vanilla
1 tablespoon raspberry liqueur (optional)
$\frac{1}{4}$ cup raspberry fruit spread
2 eggs, lightly beaten (for substitutes, see page 16)

Day before: Drain yogurt to make yogurt cheese (see p. 13).

1. Preheat oven to 325 degrees. Lightly grease a 7-inch springform pan.

2. Place yogurt cheese in a medium-size bowl. Add the cornstarch, vanilla, and liqueur, stirring gently with a fork or wire whisk until well blended. Stir in the eggs.

3. Pour half of this mixture into the prepared pan. Spread with raspberry spread. Cover with remaining yogurt mixture. With a knife, cut through the cheesecake to form a swirl. Smooth the top with a spatula. Bake until center is set, about 45 to 55 minutes.

4. Cool slightly on a wire rack. Refrigerate until chilled.

Serves 8.

Per serving: Calories 107; Protein 6 gm; Carbohydrates 14 gm; Fat 3 gm; Cholesterol 71 mg; Calcium 127 mg; Sodium 57 mg

Rothschild Cheesecake

32-ounce carton vanilla-flavored lowfat yogurt
$1/2$ cup candied mixed fruit
2 tablespooons brandy
$1/4$ cup sugar
2 tablespoons cornstarch
2 eggs, lightly beaten (for substitutes, see page 16)

Day before: Drain yogurt to make yogurt cheese (see p. 13).

1. Preheat oven to 325 degrees. Lightly grease an 8-inch pie pan or 7-inch springform pan.

2. Soak fruit in brandy for 20 minutes.

3. Place yogurt cheese in a medium-size bowl. Add sugar, cornstarch, and fruit mixture, stirring gently with a fork until well blended. Stir in the eggs.

4. Pour into the prepared pan and smooth the top with a spatula. Bake until center is set: 25 to 30 minutes for a pie pan, or 55 to 60 minutes for a springform.

5. Cool slightly on a wire rack. Refrigerate until chilled.

    Serves 8.

Per serving: Calories 159; Protein 6 gm; Carbohydrates 24 gm; Fat 3 gm; Cholesterol 71 mg; Calcium 135 mg; Sodium 74 mg

Grape-Nuts Cheesecake

32-ounce carton vanilla-flavored lowfat yogurt
¹/₄ cup sugar
1 tablespoon cornstarch
¹/₃ cup Grape-Nuts cereal
1 teaspoon vanilla
2 eggs, lightly beaten (for substitutes, see page 16)

Day before: Drain yogurt to make yogurt cheese (see p. 13).

1. Preheat oven to 325 degrees. Lightly grease an 8-inch pie pan or 7-inch springform pan.

2. Place yogurt cheese in a medium-size bowl. Add the sugar, cornstarch, Grape-Nuts, and vanilla, mixing gently with a fork or wire whisk until well blended. Stir in the eggs.

3. Pour into the prepared pan and smooth the top with a spatula. Bake until center is set: 20 to 25 minutes for a pie pan, or 45 to 55 minutes for a springform.

4. Cool slightly on a wire rack. Refrigerate until chilled.

    Serves 8.

Per serving: Calories 128; Protein 6 gm; Carbohydrates 18 gm; Fat 3 gm; Cholesterol 71 mg; Calcium 129 mg; Sodium 90 mg

Ginger Cheesecake

32-ounce carton vanilla-flavored lowfat yogurt
$1/4$ cup sugar
2 tablespoons brown sugar
1 tablespoon cornstarch
1 tablespoon lemon juice
$1/2$ teaspoon juice from grated ginger root
2 tablespoons candied ginger, finely chopped
2 eggs, lightly beaten (for substitutes, see page 16)

Day before: Drain yogurt to make yogurt cheese (see p. 13).

1. Preheat oven to 325 degrees. Lightly grease an 8-inch pie pan or 7-inch springform pan. Place grated ginger root in sieve, pressing with a spoon to extract juice.

2. Place yogurt cheese in a medium-size bowl. Add sugars, cornstarch, ginger juice, chopped candied ginger, and lemon juice, mixing gently with a fork or wire whisk until well blended. Stir in the eggs.

3. Pour into the prepared pan and smooth the top with a spatula. Bake until center is set, about 30 minutes for a pie pan, or 45 to 55 minutes for a springform.

4. Cool slightly on a wire rack. Refrigerate until chilled.

   Serves 8.

Per serving: Calories 135; Protein 6 gm; Carbohydrates 20 gm; Fat 3 gm; Cholesterol 71 mg; Calcium 130 mg; Sodium 58 mg

Pecan-Praline Cheesecake

32-ounce carton vanilla-flavored lowfat yogurt
$1/4$ cup dark brown sugar
2 tablespoons cornstarch
1 teaspoon vanilla
2 eggs, lightly beaten (for substitutes, see page 16)
$1/2$ cup chopped pecans

Day before: Drain yogurt to make yogurt cheese (see p. 13).

1. Preheat oven to 325 degrees. Lightly grease an 8-inch pie pan or 7-inch springform pan.

2. Place yogurt cheese in a medium-size bowl. Add sugar, cornstarch, and vanilla, mixing gently with a fork or wire whisk until well blended. Stir in the eggs, then the pecans.

3. Pour into the prepared pan and smooth the top with a spatula. Bake until center is set: 25 to 30 minutes for a pie pan, or 55 to 60 minutes for a springform.

4. Cool slightly on a wire rack. Refrigerate until chilled.

    Serves 8.

Per serving: Calories 162; Protein 6 gm; Carbohydrates 17 gm; Fat 8 gm; Cholesterol 71 mg; Calcium 135 mg; Sodium 59 mg

Maple Walnut Cheesecake

32-ounce carton vanilla-flavored lowfat yogurt
$1/4$ cup pure maple syrup
2 tablespoons cornstarch
$3/4$ teaspoon maple extract (optional)
$1/2$ teaspoon vanilla
2 eggs, lightly beaten (for substitutes, see page 16)
$1/2$ cup chopped walnuts

Day before: Drain yogurt to make yogurt cheese (see p. 13).

1. Preheat oven to 325 degrees. Lightly grease an 8-inch pie pan or 7-inch springform pan.

2. Place yogurt cheese in a medium-size bowl. Add syrup, cornstarch, maple extract, and vanilla extract, mixing gently with a fork or wire whisk until well blended. Stir in the eggs, then the walnuts.

3. Pour into the prepared pan and smooth the top with a spatula. Bake until center is firm: 25 to 30 minutes for a pie pan, or 55 to 60 minutes for a springform.

4. Cool slightly on a wire rack. Refrigerate until chilled.

    Serves 8.

Per serving: Calories 162; Protein 7 gm; Carbohydrates 16 gm; Fat 8 gm; Cholesterol 71 mg; Calcium 144 mg; Sodium 59 mg

Coconut Cheesecake

32-ounce carton vanilla-flavored lowfat yogurt
$1/4$ cup sugar
2 tablespoons cornstarch
2 tablespoons cream of coconut (non-alcoholic drink mix), optional
$1/2$ cup shredded coconut, toasted if desired
$1/2$ teaspoon coconut flavoring (optional)
2 eggs, lightly beaten (for substitutes, see page 16)

Day before: Drain yogurt to make yogurt cheese (see p. 13).

1. Preheat oven to 325 degrees. Lightly grease an 8-inch pie pan or 7-inch springform pan.

2. Place yogurt cheese in a medium-size bowl. Add sugar, cornstarch, coconut cream, coconut, and flavoring, mixing gently with a fork or wire whisk until well blended. Stir in the eggs.

3. Pour into the prepared pan and smooth the top with a spatula. Bake until center is set: 25 to 30 minutes for a pie pan, or 55 to 60 minutes for a springform.

4. Cool slightly on a wire rack. Refrigerate until chilled.

    Serves 8.

Per serving: Calories 142; Protein 6 gm; Carbohydrates 17 gm; Fat 5 gm; Cholesterol 71 mg; Calcium 128 mg; Sodium 73 mg

Marble Cheesecake

32-ounce carton vanilla-flavored lowfat yogurt
1 teaspoon vanilla
1 teaspoon orange liqueur (optional)
¼ cup unsweetened cocoa
3 tablespoons sugar, divided
1 tablespoon cornstarch
1 tablespoon coffee liqueur
2 eggs, lightly beaten (for substitutes, see page 16)

Day before: Drain yogurt to make yogurt cheese (see p. 13).

1. Preheat oven to 325 degrees. Lightly grease a 7-inch springform pan.

2. In a small bowl, mix ¼ cup yogurt cheese with vanilla, orange liqueur, cocoa, and 1 tablespoon sugar. Set aside.

3. In a medium bowl, combine remaining yogurt cheese with cornstarch, coffee liqueur, and remaining sugar, stirring gently with a fork or wire whisk until well blended. Stir in eggs. Pour into the pan.

4. Pour chocolate mixture into center of cheesecake in the pan. With a knife, cut through the chocolate to form a swirl while leaving most of the chocolate in the center. Bake until center is set, about 45 to 55 minutes.

5. Cool slightly on a wire rack. Refrigerate until chilled.

Serves 8.

Per serving: Calories 119; Protein 6 gm; Carbohydrates 15 gm; Fat 4 gm; Cholesterol 71 mg; Calcium 130 mg; Sodium 57 mg

Chocolate Mint Cheesecake

32-ounce carton vanilla-flavored lowfat yogurt
5 tablespoons sugar
2 tablespoons cornstarch
$\frac{1}{4}$ cup unsweetened cocoa
1 tablespoon creme de menthe
$\frac{1}{4}$ to $\frac{1}{2}$ teaspoon mint extract
2 eggs, lightly beaten (for substitutes, see page 16)

Day before: Drain yogurt (see instructions on page 13.)

1. Preheat oven to 325 degrees. Lightly grease an 8-inch pie pan or 7-inch springform pan.

2. Place yogurt cheese in a medium-size bowl. Add sugar, cornstarch, cocoa, creme de menthe, and mint extract, stirring gently with a fork or wire whisk until well blended. Stir in the eggs.

3. Pour into the prepared pan and smooth the top with a spatula. Bake until center is set: 25 to 30 minutes for a pie pan, or 55 to 60 minutes for a springform.

4. Cool slightly on a wire rack. Refrigerate until chilled.

    Serves 8.

Per serving: Calories 134; Protein 6 gm; Carbohydrates 19 gm; Fat 4 gm; Cholesterol 71 mg; Calcium 130 mg; Sodium 57 mg

Amaretto Cheesecake

32-ounce carton vanilla-flavored lowfat yogurt
1/4 cup sugar
2 tablespoons cornstarch
1/2 teaspoon vanilla
1/2 teaspoon almond extract
1 tablespoon Amaretto liqueur
2 eggs, lightly beaten (for substitutes, see page 16)

Day before: Drain yogurt (see instructions on page 13).

1. Preheat oven to 325 degrees. Lightly grease an 8-inch pie pan or 7-inch springform pan.

2. Place yogurt cheese in a medium-size bowl. Add sugar, cornstarch, vanilla, almond extract, and Amaretto, stirring gently with a fork or wire whisk until well blended. Stir in the eggs.

3. Pour into the prepared pan and smooth the top with a spatula. Bake until center is set: 25 to 30 minutes for a pie pan, or 55 to 60 minutes for a springform.

4. Cool slightly on a wire rack. Refrigerate until chilled.

Serves 8.

Per serving: Calories 121; Protein 6 gm; Carbohydrates 15 gm; Fat 3 gm; Cholesterol 71 mg; Calcium 127 mg; Sodium 57 mg

Irish Coffee Cheesecake

32-ounce carton vanilla-flavored lowfat yogurt
¼ cup sugar
2 tablespoons cornstarch
1 tablespoon instant espresso powder
3 tablespoons Irish whiskey (1 miniature bottle)
½ teaspoon vanilla
2 eggs, lightly beaten (for substitutes, see page 16)

Day before: Drain yogurt (see instructions on page 13).

1. Preheat oven to 325 degrees. Lightly grease an 8-inch pie pan or 7-inch springform pan. Dissolve espresso powder in Irish whiskey.

2. Place yogurt cheese in a medium-size bowl and stir in espresso mixture, sugar, cornstarch, and vanilla, mixing gently with a fork or wire whisk until well blended. Stir in the eggs.

3. Pour into the prepared pan and smooth the top with a spatula. Bake until center is set: 25 to 30 minutes for a pie pan, or 55 to 60 minutes for a springform.

4. Cool slightly on a wire rack. Refrigerate until chilled.

Serves 8.

Per serving: Calories 128; Protein 6 gm; Carbohydrates 15 gm; Fat 3 gm; Cholesterol 71 mg; Calcium 134 mg; Sodium 58 mg

43

Rum Raisin Cheesecake

32-ounce carton vanilla-flavored lowfat yogurt
$1/4$ cup sugar
2 tablespoons cornstarch
1 tablespoon rum
$1/4$ teaspoon rum flavoring (optional)
$1/2$ teaspoon vanilla
$1/4$ cup dark raisins
$1/4$ cup golden raisins
2 eggs, lightly beaten (for substitutes, see page 16)

Day before: Drain yogurt (see instructions on page 13).

1. Preheat oven to 325 degrees. Lightly grease an 8-inch pie pan or 7-inch springform pan.

2. Place yogurt cheese in a medium-size bowl. Add sugar, cornstarch, rum, vanilla, rum flavoring, and raisins, mixing gently with a fork or wire whisk until well blended. Stir in the eggs.

3. Pour into the prepared pan and smooth the top with a spatula. Bake until center is set: 25 to 30 minutes for a pie pan, or 55 to 60 minutes for a springform.

4. Cool slightly on a wire rack. Refrigerate until chilled.

Serves 8.

Per serving: Calories 149; Protein 6 gm; Carbohydrates 23 gm; Fat 3 gm; Cholesterol 71 mg; Calcium 134 mg; Sodium 58 mg

Chapter 2

Baked Pies

French Cherry Pie

16-ounce carton vanilla-flavored lowfat yogurt
2 tablespoons sugar
2 tablespoons cornstarch
1 package (12 oz) frozen dark sweet cherries, thawed
2 eggs, lightly beaten (for substitutes, see page 16)

Day before: Drain yogurt (see instructions on page 13).

1. Preheat oven to 325 degrees. Lightly grease a 9-inch pie pan. Drain cherries well.

2. Place yogurt cheese in a medium-size bowl. Add eggs, sugar, and cornstarch, stirring gently with a fork or wire whisk until well blended. Stir in drained cherries.

3. Pour into the prepared pan and smooth the top with a spatula. Bake until center is set, about 30 minutes.

4. Cool slightly on a wire rack. Refrigerate until chilled.

    Serves 8.

Per serving: Calories 92; Protein 4 gm; Carbohydrates 13 gm; Fat 2 gm; Cholesterol 70 mg; Calcium 77 mg; Sodium 38 mg

Lemon Cheese Pie

32-ounce carton plus 8-ounce carton nonfat yogurt
1/4 cup plus 3 tablespoons sugar (or to taste)
Juice of 1 lemon
1 tablespoon cornstarch
2 eggs, lightly beaten (for substitutes, see page 16)
1 teaspoon vanilla

Day before: Drain yogurt (see instructions on page 13).

1. Preheat oven to 325 degrees. Lightly grease an 8- or 9-inch pie pan.

2. Place 1 1/2 cups yogurt cheese in a medium-size bowl. Add 1/4 cup sugar, lemon juice, and cornstarch, stirring gently with a fork or wire whisk until well mixed. Stir in the eggs.

3. Pour into the prepared pan and smooth the top with a spatula. Bake until center is firm, about 20 minutes. Remove from oven for 10 minutes to cool slightly.

4. Combine remaining yogurt cheese with remaining 3 tablespoons sugar and the vanilla. Spread on pie and bake for 5 minutes. Chill for 24 hours.

Serves 8.

Per serving: Calories 119; Protein 7 gm; Carbohydrates 18 gm; Fat 1 gm; Cholesterol 68 mg; Calcium 182 mg; Sodium 67 mg

Orange Chiffon Pie

16-ounce carton vanilla-flavored lowfat yogurt
1/3 cup orange juice
1 tablespoon lemon juice
3 egg whites
4 tablespoons sugar

Day before: Drain yogurt (see instructions on page 13).

1.   Preheat oven to 325 degrees.

2.   Place yogurt cheese in a medium-size bowl, Gradually add orange and lemon juice, stirring gently with a fork or wire whisk until well blended.

3.   In a separate bowl, beat egg whites until foamy. Gradually add sugar and continue to beat until moist, soft peaks form when beater is withdrawn. Fold into yogurt cheese mixture.

4.   Pour into a lightly greased 9-inch pie pan and bake 20 minutes. Cool slightly on a wire rack. Refrigerate until chilled.

Serves 8.

Per serving: Calories 66; Protein 3 gm; Carbohydrates 11 gm; Fat 1 gm; Cholesterol 1 mg; Calcium 62 mg; Sodium 39 mg

Golden Peach Pie

16-ounce carton vanilla-flavored lowfat yogurt
2 cups sliced peaches
2 tablespoons confectioners' sugar (or to taste)
2 tablespoons flour
1 egg, lightly beaten (for substitutes, see page 16)

Day before: Drain yogurt (see instructions on page 13).

1. Preheat oven to 300 degrees.

2. Combine peaches and sugar, and let stand for about 10 minutes. Drain well and spread in the bottom of a 9-inch pie pan. Sprinkle with flour.

3. Place yogurt cheese in a medium-size bowl, Add egg, stirring gently with a fork or wire whisk until well blended. Spread over peaches.

4. Bake for 30 minutes or until center is set. Cool slightly on a wire rack. Refrigerate until chilled.

    Serves 8.

Per serving: Calories 73; Protein 3 gm; Carbohydrates 11 gm; Fat 2 gm; Cholesterol 36 mg; Calcium 66 mg; Sodium 29 mg

Peach Cream Pie

32-ounce carton vanilla-flavored lowfat yogurt
20 ounces sliced peaches (frozen or canned)
$^2/_3$ cup peach liquid or water
2 tablespoons quick-cooking tapioca
2 egg whites
2 tablespoons sugar

Day before: Drain yogurt (see instructions on page 13).

1. Preheat oven to 325 degrees. Lightly grease a 9-inch pie pan.

2. Drain peaches, reserving liquid. Add water to equal $^2/_3$ cup liquid. Combine liquid and tapioca in a saucepan. Set aside for 5 minutes. Then cook over low heat until slightly thickened, about 5 minutes. Cool slightly.

3. Place yogurt cheese in a medium-size bowl. Gradually add tapioca mixture, stirring gently until well blended.

4. In a separate bowl, beat the egg whites until foamy. Gradually add sugar and continue to beat until moist, soft peaks form when beater is withdrawn. Fold into yogurt cheese mixture.

5. Pour half the mixture into the prepared pan, cover with a layer of peaches, and top with remaining mixture. Bake until set, about 40 minutes.

6. Cool slightly on a wire rack. Refrigerate until chilled.

    Serves 8.

    Per serving: Calories 118; Protein 6 gm; Carbohydrates 20 gm; Fat 2 gm; Cholesterol 3 mg; Calcium 126 mg; Sodium 56 mg

Raspberry Cream Pie

32-ounce carton vanilla-flavored lowfat yogurt
²/₃ cup orange juice
2 tablespoons quick-cooking tapioca
2 egg whites
2 tablespoons sugar
1 package (12 oz) frozen raspberries, thawed and drained

Day before: Drain yogurt (see instructions on page 13).

1. Preheat oven to 325 degrees. Lightly grease a 9-inch pie pan.

2. Combine orange juice and tapioca in a saucepan, and set aside for 5 minutes. Then cook over low heat until slightly thickened, about 5 minutes. Cool slightly.

3. Place yogurt cheese in a medium-size bowl. Gradually add tapioca mixture, stirring gently with a fork or wire whisk.

4. In a separate bowl, beat egg whites until foamy. Gradually add sugar and continue to beat until moist, soft peaks form when beater is withdrawn. Fold into yogurt cheese mixture.

5. Pour half the mixture into the prepared pan. Add a layer of raspberries. Cover with remaining mixture and bake until set, about 40 minutes.

6. Cool slightly on a wire rack. Refrigerate until chilled.

Serves 8.

Per serving: Calories 111; Protein 6 gm; Carbohydrates 18 gm; Fat 2 gm; Cholesterol 3 mg; Calcium 138 mg; Sodium 52 mg

Rhubarb Cream Pie

32-ounce carton vanilla-flavored lowfat yogurt
2 cups frozen cut rhubarb (unsweetened), thawed
1 jar (6 oz) strained bananas (baby food)
$1/4$ cup confectioners' sugar
3 tablespoons cornstarch
2 eggs, lightly beaten (for substitutes, see page 16)

Day before: Drain yogurt (see instructions on page 13).

1. Combine drained rhubarb and banana and set aside for about 30 minutes. Preheat oven to 325 degrees. Lightly grease a 9-inch pie pan.

2. Place yogurt cheese in a medium-size bowl. Add the cornstarch and sugar, stirring gently with a fork or wire whisk until well blended. Stir in the eggs. Fold in rhubarb mixture.

3. Pour into a 9-inch pie pan and smooth the top with a spatula. Bake until center is set, about 30 to 35 minutes.

4. Cool slightly on a wire rack. Refrigerate until chilled.

    Serves 8.

Per serving: Calories 126; Protein 6 gm; Carbohydrates 18 gm; Fat 3 gm; Cholesterol 71 mg; Calcium 154 mg; Sodium 61 mg

Strawberry Cream Pie I

32-ounce carton vanilla-flavored lowfat yogurt
²/₃ cup orange juice
2 tablespoons quick-cooking tapioca
1 pint fresh strawberries, sliced
2 egg whites
2 tablespoons sugar

Day before: Drain yogurt (see instructions on page 13).

1. Preheat oven to 325 degrees. Lightly grease a 9-inch pie pan.

2. Combine orange juice and tapioca in a saucepan and set aside for 5 minutes. Then cook over low heat until slightly thickened, about 5 minutes. Cool slightly.

3. Place yogurt cheese in a medium-size bowl. Gradually add tapioca mixture, stirring gently with a fork or wire whisk until well blended. Fold in strawberries.

4. In separate bowl, beat egg whites until foamy. Gradually add sugar and continue to beat until moist, soft peaks form when beater is withdrawn. Fold into yogurt cheese mixture.

5. Pour into the prepared pan and bake until set, about 40 minutes. Cool slightly on a wire rack. Refrigerate until chilled.

    Serves 8.

Per serving: Calories 106; Protein 6 gm; Carbohydrates 17 gm; Fat 2 gm; Cholesterol 3 mg; Calcium 128 mg; Sodium 53 mg

Strawberry Cream Pie II

32-ounce carton vanilla-flavored lowfat yogurt
$2/3$ cup orange juice
2 tablespoons quick-cooking tapioca
$1/4$ cup strawberry fruit spread
2 egg whites
2 tablespoons sugar

Day before: Drain yogurt (see instructions on page 13).

1. Preheat oven to 325 degrees. Lightly grease a 9-inch pie pan.

2. Combine orange juice and tapioca in a saucepan and set aside for 5 minutes. Then cook over low heat until slightly thickened, about 5 minutes. Cool slightly.

3. Place yogurt cheese in a medium-size bowl. Gradually add tapioca mixture and strawberry spread, stirring gently with a fork or wire whisk until well blended.

4. In a separate bowl, beat the egg whites until foamy. Gradually add sugar and continue to beat until moist, soft peaks form when beater is withdrawn. Fold into yogurt cheese mixture.

5. Pour into the prepared pan and bake until set, about 40 minutes. Cool slightly on a wire rack. Refrigerate until chilled.

    Serves 8.

Per serving: Calories 116; Protein 5 gm; Carbohydrates 20 gm; Fat 2 gm; Cholesterol 3 mg; Calcium 123 mg; Sodium 52 mg

Carrot Pie

16-ounce carton vanilla-flavored lowfat yogurt
1 1/2 cups sliced carrots
2 tablespoons sugar (or more to taste)
1 tablespoon cornstarch
1 teaspoon cinnamon
1/2 teaspoon ground ginger
1/2 teaspoon vanilla
2 eggs, lightly beaten (for substitutes, see page 16)

Day before: Drain yogurt (see instructions on page 13).

1. Preheat oven to 325 degrees. Lightly grease a 9-inch pie pan.

2. Cook carrots until tender. Drain. Puree in a food mill or food processor.

3. Place yogurt cheese in a medium-size bowl. Add the sugar, cornstarch, cinnamon, ginger, and vanilla, stirring gently with a fork or wire whisk until well blended. Fold in carrots. Stir in the eggs.

4. Pour into the prepared pan and smooth the top with a spatula. Bake until center is set, 20 to 25 minutes. Cool slightly on a wire rack and refrigerate until chilled.

    Serves 8.

Per serving: Calories 81; Protein 4 gm; Carbohydrates 11 gm; Fat 2 gm; Cholesterol 70 mg; Calcium 80 mg; Sodium 57 mg

Pumpkin Pie

32-ounce carton vanilla-flavored lowfat yogurt
³/₄ cup sugar (or to taste)
2 tablespoons cornstarch
1 cup pumpkin puree
1 teaspoon cinnamon
¹/₂ teaspoon ground ginger
¹/₄ teaspoon ground cloves
2 eggs, lightly beaten (for substitutes, see page 16)

Day before: Drain yogurt (see instructions on page 13).

1. Preheat oven to 300 degrees. Lightly grease a 9-inch pie pan.

2. Place yogurt cheese in a medium-size bowl. Add the sugar, cornstarch, pumpkin, cinnamon, ginger, and cloves, mixing gently with a fork or wire whisk until well blended. Stir in the eggs.

3. Pour into the prepared pan and smooth the top with a spatula. Bake until center is set, about 1 hour.

4. Cool slightly on a wire rack. Refrigerate until chilled.

Serves 8.

Per serving: Calories 172; Protein 6 gm; Carbohydrates 30 gm; Fat 3 gm; Cholesterol 71 mg; Calcium 138 mg; Sodium 59 mg

Raisin Pie

16-ounce carton vanilla-flavored lowfat yogurt
1 cup seedless raisins
$^{1}/_{2}$ cup water
2 tablespoons cornstarch
$^{1}/_{4}$ teaspoon ground cloves
$^{1}/_{4}$ teaspoon cinnamon
1 egg, lightly beaten (for substitutes, see page 16)

Day before: Drain yogurt (see instructions on page 13).

1. Preheat oven to 325 degrees. Lightly grease a 9-inch pie pan.

2. In a covered saucepan, cook raisins in water until plump. Drain well. Place the yogurt cheese in a medium-size bowl. Add cornstarch, cloves, and cinnamon, stirring gently with a fork or wire whisk until well blended. Stir in egg. Fold in raisins.

3. Pour into the prepared pan and smooth the top with a spatula. Bake until center is set, about 30 minutes.

4. Cool slightly on a wire rack. Refrigerate until chilled.

    Serves 8.

Per serving: Calories 110; Protein 4 gm; Carbohydrates 21 gm; Fat 2 gm; Cholesterol 36 mg; Calcium 75 mg; Sodium 31 mg

Butternut Squash Pie

32-ounce carton vanilla-flavored lowfat yogurt
1 two-pound butternut squash
$1/4$ cup sugar
2 tablespoons cornstarch
1 teaspoon cinnamon
1 teaspoon ground ginger
2 eggs, lightly beaten (for substitutes, see page 16)

Day before: Drain yogurt (see instructions on page 13).

1. Preheat oven to 325 degrees. Lightly grease a 9-inch pie pan.

2. Cut squash into chunks and steam for 20 minutes or until tender. Cut away skin and discard seeds. Puree squash.

3. Place yogurt cheese in a medium-size bowl. Add the sugar, cornstarch, cinnamon, ginger, and 2 cups of squash, mixing gently with a fork or wire whisk until well blended. Stir in the eggs.

4. Pour into the prepared pan and smooth the top with a spatula. Bake until center is set, about 1 hour. Cool slightly on a wire rack. Refrigerate until chilled.

Serves 8.

Per serving: Calories 135; Protein 6 gm; Carbohydrates 20 gm; Fat 3 gm; Cholesterol 71 mg; Calcium 152 mg; Sodium 60 mg

Chocolate Cream Pie

32-ounce carton vanilla-flavored lowfat yogurt
$2/3$ cup orange juice
6 tablespoons cocoa
2 tablespoons quick-cooking tapioca
2 egg whites
2 tablespoons sugar

Day before: Drain yogurt (see instructions on page 13).

1. Preheat oven to 325 degrees. Lightly grease a 9-inch pie pan.

2. Combine orange juice, cocoa, and tapioca in a saucepan, and set aside for 5 minutes. Then cook over low heat until slightly thickened, about 5 minutes. Cool slightly.

3. Place yogurt cheese in a medium-size bowl. Gradually add tapioca mixture, stirring gently with a fork or wire whisk until well mixed.

4. In a separate bowl, beat the egg whites until foamy. Gradually add sugar and continue to beat until moist, soft peaks form when beater is withdrawn. Fold into yogurt cheese mixture.

5. Pour into the prepared pan and bake until set, about 40 minutes. Cool slightly on a wire rack. Refrigerate until chilled.

Serves 8.

Per serving: Calories 106; Protein 6 gm; Carbohydrates 16 gm; Fat 3 gm; Cholesterol 3 mg; Calcium 128 mg; Sodium 52 mg

Chapter 3

No-Bake Pies

Apricot Chiffon Pie

32-ounce carton vanilla-flavored lowfat yogurt
4 jars (4 $\frac{1}{2}$ oz each) strained apricots (baby food)
$\frac{1}{4}$ cup sugar, or to taste
2 tablespoons unflavored gelatin
$\frac{3}{4}$ cups cold water, divided
2 tablespoons lemon juice

Day before: Drain yogurt (see instructions on page 13).

1. In a large bowl, combine apricots, sugar and yogurt cheese, stirring gently with a fork or wire whisk until well blended.

2. Soften gelatin in $\frac{1}{4}$ cup water for 5 minutes. In a saucepan, heat remaining water and lemon juice. Add gelatin and stir until dissolved. Pour into a mixing bowl and refrigerate for 10 minutes.

3. Whip gelatin mixture with an electric beater on high speed until foamy and thick, about 1 to $1\frac{1}{2}$ minutes. Do not overbeat. Fold into yogurt cheese mixture.

4. Pour into a 10-inch piepan and chill until set (about 3 hours).

    Serves 8.

Per serving: Calories 133; Protein 6 gm; Carbohydrates 23 gm; Fat 2 gm; Cholesterol 3 mg; Calcium 127 mg; Sodium 47 mg

Banana Chiffon Pie

32-ounce carton vanilla-flavored lowfat yogurt
1 cup mashed bananas
$^1/_2$ cup lemon juice, divided
$^1/_4$ cup sugar, or to taste
2 tablespoons unflavored gelatin
$^3/_4$ cup water, divided

Day before: Drain yogurt (see instructions on page 13).

1. In a large bowl, combine bananas and $^1/_4$ cup lemon juice. Add sugar and yogurt cheese, stirring gently with a fork or wire whisk until well blended. Set aside.

2. Soften gelatin in $^1/_4$ cup water for 5 minutes. In a saucepan, heat remaining water and $^1/_4$ cup lemon juice. Add gelatin and stir until dissolved. Pour into a mixing bowl and refrigerate for 10 minutes.

3. Whip gelatin mixture with an electric beater on high speed until foamy and thick, about 1 to $1^1/_2$ minutes. Do not overbeat. Fold into gelatin mixture.

4. Pour into a 9-inch pie pan and chill until set (about 3 hours).

    Serves 8.

Per serving: Calories 132; Protein 7 gm; Carbohydrates 23 gm; Fat 2 gm; Cholesterol 3 mg; Calcium 123 mg; Sodium 43 mg

Banana Cream Pie

32-ounce carton nonfat yogurt
2 teaspoons vanilla
1/4 cup confectioners' sugar (or to taste)
2 large bananas
1 tablespoon lemon juice

Day before: Drain yogurt (see instructions on page 13).

1. Place yogurt cheese in a medium-size bowl. Add the vanilla and sugar, stirring gently with a fork or wire whisk until well mixed.

2. Slice bananas and toss lightly with lemon juice. Alternate layers of bananas and yogurt cheese in a 9-inch pie pan, ending with a layer of yogurt cheese. Chill several hours before serving.

    Serves 8.

Per serving: Calories 112; Protein 5 gm; Carbohydrates 22 gm; Fat <1 gm; Cholesterol 0 mg; Calcium 144 mg; Sodium 40 mg

French Blueberry Pie

32-ounce carton vanilla-flavored lowfat yogurt
1/4 cup confectioners' sugar
1 pint fresh blueberries
1 tablespoon cornstarch
1/4 cup sugar
1/2 cup water

Day before: Drain yogurt (see instructions on page 13).

1.   Place yogurt cheese in a medium-size bowl. Add confectioners' sugar, mixing gently with a fork or wire whisk until well blended. Spread in a smooth layer in the bottom of a 9-inch pie pan. Chill.

2.   Wash and drain blueberries. In a medium-size pan, combine half of the berries with cornstarch, sugar, and 1/2 cup water. Cook, stirring gently, until sauce thickens. Fold in remaining berries.

3.   Spread blueberries over the cheese layer. Refrigerate until chilled.

Serves 8.

Per serving: Calories 126; Protein 5 gm; Carbohydrates 23 gm; Fat 2 gm; Cholesterol 3 mg; Calcium 122 mg; Sodium 42 mg

Mandarin Blueberry Pie

32-ounce carton vanilla-flavored lowfat yogurt
1 can (11 oz) mandarin oranges
2 tablespoons unflavored gelatin
1 ½ cups orange juice
2 tablespoons confectioners' sugar
1 pint fresh blueberries

Day before: Drain yogurt (see instructions on page 13).

1. Drain mandarin oranges, reserving liquid. In a small saucepan, soften gelatin in mandarin orange liquid for 5 minutes. Place over low heat and stir until gelatin dissolves. Stir in orange juice. Chill until slightly thickened.

2. Combine blueberries and sugar. Set aside.

3. Place yogurt cheese in a medium-size bowl. Gradually add gelatin mixture and stir with a fork or wire whisk until well blended. Fold in oranges and blueberries.

4. Pour into a 9-inch pie pan. Chill several hours or until set.

Serves 8.

Per serving: Calories 132; Protein 7 gm; Carbohydrates 22 gm; Fat 2 gm; Cholesterol 3 mg; Calcium 131 mg; Sodium 46 mg

Really Creamy Cherry Pie

16-ounce carton vanilla-flavored lowfat yogurt
¼ cup confectioners' sugar
1 package (12 oz) frozen dark sweet cherries, thawed
2 tablespoons cornstarch
2 tablespoons sugar

Day before: Drain yogurt (see instructions on page 13).

1. Place yogurt cheese in a medium-size bowl. Add confectioners' sugar, stirring gently with a fork or wire whisk until well blended. Spread in a smooth layer on the bottom of a 9-inch pie pan. Chill.

2. Drain cherries, reserving liquid. In a medium-size saucepan, mix cherry liquid with cornstarch and sugar, and cook until slightly thickened. Add cherries and cook, gently stirring, for a few minutes. Cool slightly.

3. Spread berries over cheese layer. Chill and serve.

    Serves 8.

Per serving: Calories 88; Protein 3 gm; Carbohydrates 17 gm; Fat 1 gm; Cholesterol 1 mg; Calcium 70 mg; Sodium 21 mg

Cranberry Bavarian Pie

32-ounce carton vanilla-flavored lowfat yogurt
$1/4$ cup water
2 tablespoons unflavored gelatin
1 can (16 oz) jellied cranberry sauce

Day before: Drain yogurt (see instructions on page 13).

1. Soften gelatin in $1/4$ cup water for 5 minutes. Heat cranberries over low heat until melted. Add gelatin and stir until dissolved. Cool slightly.

2. Place yogurt cheese in a medium-size bowl. Gradually add cranberry mixture, mixing gently with a fork or wire whisk until well blended.

3. Pour into a 9-inch pie pan. Refrigerate until firm.

    Serves 8.

Per serving: Calories 150; Protein 6 gm; Carbohydrates 28 gm; Fat 2 gm; Cholesterol 3 mg; Calcium 123 mg; Sodium 43 mg

Grape Chiffon Pie

32-ounce carton vanilla-flavored lowfat yogurt
1 1/2 tablespoons unflavored gelatin
1 cup grape juice, divided

Day before: Drain yogurt (see instructions on page 13).

1. Place yogurt cheese in a large bowl and stir gently with a fork or wire whisk.

2. Soften gelatin in 1/4 cup grape juice for 5 minutes. In a saucepan, heat remaining juice. Add gelatin and stir until dissolved. Pour into a mixing bowl and refrigerate for 10 minutes.

3. Whip gelatin mixture with an electric beater until foamy and thick, about 1 minute to 1 1/2 minutes. Do not over-beat. Fold into yogurt cheese.

4. Pour into a 10-inch pie pan and chill until set (about 3 hours).

    Serves 8.

Per serving: Calories 87; Protein 6 gm; Carbohydrates 11 gm; Fat 2 gm; Cholesterol 3 mg; Calcium 123 mg; Sodium 43 mg

Grapefruit Chiffon Pie

32-ounce carton vanilla-flavored lowfat yogurt
1 tablespoon lemon juice
$^1/_4$ cup sugar, or to taste
$1^1/_2$ tablespoons unflavored gelatin
$^3/_4$ cup cold water, divided
$^1/_4$ cup grapefruit juice

Day before: Drain yogurt (see instructions on page 13).

1. In a large bowl, combine lemon juice, sugar, and yogurt cheese, stirring gently with a fork or wire whisk until well blended.

2. Soften gelatin in $^1/_4$ cup water for 5 minutes. In a saucepan, heat remaining water and grapefruit juice. Add gelatin and stir until dissolved. Pour into a mixing bowl and refrigerate for 10 minutes.

3. Whip gelatin mixture with an electric beater on high speed until foamy and thick, about 1 to $1^1/_2$ minutes. Do not overbeat. Fold into yogurt cheese mixture.

4. Pour into a 9-inch pie pan and chill until set (about 3 hours).

    Serves 8.

Per serving: Calories 95; Protein 6 gm; Carbohydrates 14 gm; Fat 2 gm; Cholesterol 3 mg; Calcium 121 mg; Sodium 42 mg

Key Lime Pie

32-ounce carton vanilla-flavored lowfat yogurt
$1/3$ cup confectioners' sugar (or to taste)
$1/4$ cup key lime juice

Day before: Drain yogurt (see instructions on page 13).

1. Place yogurt cheese in a medium-size bowl. Add sugar and lime juice, stirring gently with a fork or wire whisk until well blended.

2. Pour into a 9-inch pie pan. Chill 24 hours before serving.

    Serves 8.

Per serving: Calories 88; Protein 4 gm; Carbohydrates 13 gm; Fat 2 gm; Cholesterol 3 mg; Calcium 121 mg; Sodium 41 mg

Lemon Chiffon Pie

32-ounce carton vanilla-flavored lowfat yogurt
1½ teaspoons grated lemon peel
¼ cup sugar, or to taste
1½ tablespoons unflavored gelatin
¾ cup cold water
¼ cup plus 1 tablespoon lemon juice

Day before: Drain yogurt (see instructions on page 13).

1. In a large bowl, combine lemon peel, sugar and yogurt cheese, stirring gently with a fork or wire whisk until well blended.

2. Soften gelatin in ¼ cup water for 5 minutes. In a saucepan, heat lemon juice and remaining water. Add gelatin and stir until dissolved. Pour into a mixing bowl and refrigerate for 10 minutes.

3. Whip gelatin mixture with an electric beater until foamy and thick, about 1 to 1½ minutes. Do not overbeat. Fold into yogurt cheese mixture.

4. Pour into a 9-inch pie pan and chill until set (about 3 hours).

Serves 8.

Per serving: Calories 94; Protein 6 gm; Carbohydrates 14 gm; Fat 2 gm; Cholesterol 3 mg; Calcium 121 mg; Sodium 42 mg

Pineapple Chiffon Pie

32-ounce carton vanilla-flavored lowfat yogurt
1 can (20 oz) crushed pineapple, packed in own juice
1 tablespoon lemon juice
2 tablespoons unflavored gelatin

Day before: Drain yogurt (see instructions on page 13).

1. Drain pineapple, reserving 1 cup juice (or add water to equal 1 cup).

2. In a large bowl, combine crushed pineapple, lemon juice, and yogurt cheese, stirring gently with a fork or wire whisk until well blended. Set aside.

3. Soften gelatin in $1/4$ cup pineapple juice for 5 minutes. Pour remaining juice into a saucepan. Heat, then add softened gelatin and stir until gelatin is dissolved. Pour into a mixing bowl and refrigerate for 10 minutes.

4. Whip gelatin mixture with an electric beater on high speed until foamy and thick, about 1 to $1^1/_2$ minutes. Do not overbeat. Fold into yogurt cheese mixture.

5. Pour into a 10-inch pie pan and chill until set (about 3 hours).

   Serves 8.

Per serving: Calories 113; Protein 7 gm; Carbohydrates 18 gm; Fat 2 gm; Cholesterol 3 mg; Calcium 130 mg; Sodium 44 mg

Strawberry Bavarian Pie

32-ounce carton vanilla-flavored lowfat yogurt
3/4 cup water, divided
2 tablespoons unflavored gelatin
2 pints strawberries, sliced
1/4 cup sugar (or to taste)

Day before: Drain yogurt (see instructions on page 13).

1. Soften gelatin in 1/4 cup water for 5 minutes. Heat 1/2 cup water, add gelatin, and stir until dissolved. Gradually stir into sweetened strawberries.

2. Place yogurt cheese in a medium-size bowl. Add strawberry mixture, stirring gently with a fork until well blended.

3. Pour into a 9-inch pie pan. Refrigerate until firm.

    Serves 8.

Per serving: Calories 115; Protein 6 gm; Carbohydrates 18 gm; Fat 2 gm; Cholesterol 3 mg; Calcium 130 mg; Sodium 43 mg

Tropical Cream Pie

16-ounce carton nonfat yogurt
1 can (20 oz) crushed pineapple, packed in own juice
1 tablespoon unflavored gelatin
1 medium banana, chopped
1 tablespoon lemon juice
2 tablespoons confectioners' sugar
2 tablespoons flaked coconut

Day before: Drain yogurt (see instructions on page 13).

1. Drain pineapple in a strainer, pressing against sides to remove liquid (reserve liquid). Soften gelatin in ¼ cup pineapple liquid for 5 minutes. Heat ½ cup pineapple liquid; add softened gelatin and stir until dissolved. Cool slightly. Sprinkle bananas with lemon juice, and toss.

2. Place yogurt cheese in a medium-size bowl. Stir in sugar gently with a fork or wire whisk. Gradually add gelatin mixture and continue stirring until well blended. Fold in pineapple, bananas, and coconut.

3. Pour into a 9-inch pie pan. Chill several hours or until set.

    Serves 8.

Per serving: Calories 103; Protein 4 gm; Carbohydrates 22 gm; Fat 1 gm; Cholesterol 0 mg; Calcium 82 mg; Sodium 26 mg

Chocolate Chiffon Pie

32-ounce carton vanilla-flavored lowfat yogurt
$^{1}/_{3}$ cup unsweetened cocoa
1$^{1}/_{4}$ cups cold water, divided
1 teaspoon vanilla
$^{1}/_{4}$ cup sugar, or to taste
1$^{1}/_{2}$ tablespoons unflavored gelatin

Day before: Drain yogurt (see instructions on page 13).

1. In a large bowl, stir cocoa and $^{1}/_{4}$ cup water until smooth. Add vanilla, sugar, and yogurt cheese, stirring gently with a fork or wire whisk until well blended.

2. Soften gelatin in $^{1}/_{4}$ cup water for 5 minutes. In a saucepan, heat $^{3}/_{4}$ cup water. Add gelatin and stir until dissolved. Pour into a mixing bowl and refrigerate for 10 minutes.

3. Whip gelatin mixture with an electric beater on high speed until foamy and thick, about 1 to 1$^{1}/_{2}$ minutes. Do not overbeat. Fold into yogurt cheese mixture.

4. Pour into a 10-inch pie pan and chill until set (about 3 hours).

    Serves 8.

Per serving: Calories 103; Protein 6 gm; Carbohydrates 15 gm; Fat 2 gm; Cholesterol 3 mg; Calcium 125 mg; Sodium 42 mg

Coffee Chiffon Pie

32-ounce carton vanilla-flavored lowfat yogurt
2 teaspoons instant coffee powder
1 cup plus 2 tablespoons water, divided
1/4 cup sugar, or to taste
2 tablespoons unflavored gelatin

Day before: Drain yogurt (see instructions on page 13).

1. In a large bowl, dissolve coffee in 2 tablespoons hot water. Add yogurt cheese and sugar, stirring gently with a fork or wire whisk until well blended.

2. Soften gelatin in 1/4 cup cold water. In a saucepan, heat remaining water. Add gelatin and stir until dissolved. Pour into a mixing bowl and refrigerate for 10 minutes.

3. Whip gelatin mixture with an electric beater on high speed until foamy and thick, about 1 to 1 1/2 minutes. Do not overbeat. Fold into yogurt cheese mixture.

4. Pour into a 10-inch pie pan and chill until set (about 3 hours).

Serves 8.

Per serving: Calories 94; Protein 6 gm; Carbohydrates 13 gm; Fat 2 gm; Cholesterol 3 mg; Calcium 121 mg; Sodium 43 mg

Mocha Chiffon Pie

32-ounce carton vanilla-flavored lowfat yogurt
2 tablespoons unsweetened cocoa
2 teaspoons instant coffee
1 cup plus 2 tablespoons water, divided
$\frac{1}{4}$ cup sugar, or to taste
2 tablespoons unflavored gelatin

Day before: Drain yogurt (see instructions on page 13).

1. Combine cocoa and coffee. Add 2 tablespoons hot water and stir until smooth. In a large bowl, combine yogurt cheese, sugar, and cocoa mixture, stirring gently with a fork or wire whisk until well blended.

2. Soften gelatin in $\frac{1}{4}$ cup cold water for 5 minutes. In a saucepan, heat remaining water, add gelatin, and stir until dissolved. Pour into a mixing bowl and refrigerate for 10 minutes.

3. Whip gelatin mixture with an electric beater on high speed until foamy and thick, about 1 to $1\frac{1}{2}$ minutes. Do not overbeat. Fold into yogurt cheese.

4. Pour into a 10-inch pie pan and chill until set (about 3 hours).

    Serves 8.

Per serving: Calories 98; Protein 6 gm; Carbohydrates 14 gm; Fat 2 gm; Cholesterol 3 mg; Calcium 122 mg; Sodium 43 mg

Rum Chiffon Pie

32-ounce carton vanilla-flavored lowfat yogurt
2 tablespoons dark rum (or 2 tsp rum flavoring), or more to
taste
1 teaspoon vanilla
$^1/_4$ cup sugar, or to taste
1$^1/_2$ tablespoons gelatin
$^3/_4$ cup cold water, divided

Day before: Drain yogurt (see instructions on page 13).

1. In a large bowl, combine rum, vanilla, sugar, and yogurt
    cheese, stirring gently with a fork or wire whisk until well
    blended. Adjust flavoring if desired.

2. Soften gelatin in $^1/_4$ cup water for 5 minutes. In a sauce-
    pan, heat remaining water. Add gelatin and stir until
    dissolved. Pour into a mixing bowl and refrigerate for
    10 minutes.

3. Whip gelatin mixture with an electric beater on high
    speed until foamy and thick, about 1 to 1$^1/_2$ minutes. Do
    not overbeat. Fold into yogurt cheese mixture.

4. Pour into a 10-inch pie pan and chill until set.

    Serves 8.

Per serving: Calories 102; Protein 6 gm; Carbohydrates 13 gm;
Fat 2 gm; Cholesterol 3 mg; Calcium 124 mg; Sodium 42 mg

Coconut Cream Pie

32-ounce carton nonfat yogurt
2 teaspoons vanilla
¼ cup confectioners' sugar (or to taste)
⅓ cup flaked coconut, toasted if desired

Day before: Drain yogurt (see instructions on page 13).

1. Place yogurt cheese in a medium-size bowl. Add the vanilla and sugar, stirring gently until well mixed. Stir in coconut.

2. Pour into a 9-inch pie pan. Chill for 24 hours before serving.

    Serves 8.

Per serving: Calories 81; Protein 5 gm; Carbohydrates 11 gm; Fat 2 gm; Cholesterol 0 mg; Calcium 141 mg; Sodium 51 mg

Peanut Butter Pie

Filling: 32-ounce carton nonfat yogurt
1 teaspoon vanilla
2 tablespoons confectioners' sugar (or to taste)
3 tablespoons peanut butter (no added sugar or salt)

Crust: 4 zweiback slices
1 tablespoon peanut butter (no added sugar or salt)

Day before: Drain yogurt (see instructions on page 13).

1. Place yogurt cheese in a medium-size bowl. Add vanilla, sugar, and peanut butter, stirring gently with a fork or wire whisk until well blended.

2. Place crust ingredients in a food processor or blender and process until well blended. Press into the bottom of a 9-inch pie pan.

3. Pour filling into the crust and smooth the top with a spatula. Refrigerate 24 hours before serving.

   Serves 8.

Per serving: Calories 113; Protein 7 gm; Carbohydrates 10 gm; Fat 4 gm; Cholesterol 0 mg; Calcium 145 mg; Sodium 48 mg

Chapter 4

Mousses, Ice Creams
& Rice Puddings

Apricot Ice Cream

32-ounce carton vanilla-flavored lowfat yogurt
2 jars (4 ½ oz each) strained apricots (baby food)

Day before: Drain yogurt (see instructions on page 13).

1. Place yogurt cheese in a medium-size bowl. Add the apricots, stirring gently with a fork or wire whisk until well blended. Chill several hours to let flavors blend.

2. Process in an ice cream maker following manufacturer's instructions. If you do not have an ice cream maker, pour into an 8- or 9-inch square metal pan and freeze until firm but not hard; if frozen hard, place in refrigerator until a toothpick can be inserted (about 1 hour). Break into pieces and beat with an electric mixer until smooth. Spoon into a chilled mold and freeze.

    Note: This recipe also makes a great frozen bar. After step 1, pour into small paper cups or plastic molds.

    Serves 4.

Per serving: Calories 162; Protein 9 gm; Carbohydrates 23 gm; Fat 4 gm; Cholesterol 6 mg; Calcium 247 mg; Sodium 84 mg

Cherry Chocolate Ice Cream

32-ounce carton vanilla-flavored lowfat yogurt
1 cup frozen dark sweet cherries, thawed and drained
2 tablespoons chocolate liqueur
$1/3$ cup grated semi-sweet chocolate

Day before: Drain yogurt (see instructions on page 13).

1.   Chop or halve the cherries. Pour liqueur over cherries and macerate for 5 minutes.

2.   Place yogurt cheese in a medium-size bowl. Add cherries and chocolate, stirring gently with a fork until well blended. Chill several hours to let flavors blend.

3.   Process in an ice cream maker following manufacturer's instructions. If you do not have an ice cream maker, pour into an 8- or 9-inch square metal pan and place in freezer. About 1 hour before serving, remove from freezer and place in refrigerator.

Serves 4.

Per serving: Calories 247; Protein 10 gm; Carbohydrates 29 gm; Fat 5 gm; Cholesterol 6 mg; Calcium 253 mg; Sodium 81 mg

Ginger Ice Cream

32-ounce carton vanilla-flavored lowfat yogurt
¼ cup finely chopped candied ginger

Day before: Drain yogurt (see instructions on page 13).

1. Place yogurt cheese in a medium-size bowl. Add the chopped ginger, stirring gently with a fork or wire whisk until well blended. Chill several hours to let flavors blend.

2. Process in an ice cream maker following manufacturer's instructions. If you do not have an ice cream maker, pour into an 8- or 9-inch square metal pan and freeze until firm but not hard; if frozen hard, place in refrigerator until a toothpick can be inserted (about 1 hour). Break into pieces and beat until smooth. Spoon into a chilled mold and freeze.

Serves 4.

Per serving: Calories 172; Protein 9 gm; Carbohydrates 25 gm; Fat 4 gm; Cholesterol 6 mg; Calcium 240 mg; Sodium 80 mg

Key Lime Ice Cream

32-ounce carton vanilla-flavored lowfat yogurt
$1/4$ cup key lime juice
$1/3$ cup confectioners' sugar

Day before: Drain yogurt (see instructions on page 13).

1. Place yogurt cheese in a medium-size bowl. Add the lime juice and sugar, stirring gently with a fork or wire whisk until well blended. Chill several hours to let flavors blend.

2. Process in an ice cream maker following manufacturer's instructions. If you do not have an ice cream maker, pour into an 8- or 9-inch square metal pan and freeze until firm but not hard; if frozen hard, place in refrigerator until a toothpick can be inserted (about 1 hour). Break into pieces and beat until smooth. Spoon into a chilled mold and freeze.

    Note: This recipe also makes a great frozen bar. After step 1, pour into small paper cups or plastic molds.

    Serves 4.

Per serving: Calories 168; Protein 9 gm; Carbohydrates 25 gm; Fat 3.6 gm; Cholesterol 6 mg; Calcium 242 mg; Sodium 82 mg

Strawberry Ice Cream

32-ounce carton vanilla-flavored lowfat yogurt
2 pints strawberries, washed, hulled, and crushed

Day before: Drain yogurt (see instructions on page 13).

1. Place yogurt cheese in a medium-size bowl. Add the strawberries, stirring gently with a fork until well blended. Chill several hours to let flavors blend.

2. Process in an ice cream maker following manufacturer's instructions. If you do not have an ice cream maker, pour into a 9-inch square metal pan and freeze until firm but not hard; if frozen hard, place in refrigerator until a toothpick can be inserted (about 1 hour). Break into pieces and beat until smooth. Spoon into a chilled mold and freeze.

Note: This recipe also makes a great frozen bar. After step 1, pour into small paper cups or plastic molds.

Serves 6.

Per serving: Calories 113; Protein 6 gm; Carbohydrates 16 gm; Fat 3 gm; Cholesterol 4 mg; Calcium 174 mg; Sodium 55 mg

Easy Creamy Rice Pudding

32-ounce carton vanilla-flavored lowfat yogurt
3 cups cooked white rice (cooked without salt)
2 tablespoons strawberry fruit spread

Day before: Drain yogurt (see instructions on page 13).

1. Place yogurt cheese in a medium-size bowl. Add rice and strawberry spread, stirring gently with a fork until well blended.

2. Spoon into individual serving dishes. Refrigerate until chilled.

    Serves 8.

Per serving: Calories 156; Protein 6 gm; Carbohydrates 28 gm; Fat 2 gm; Cholesterol 3 mg; Calcium 127 mg; Sodium 41 mg

Cinnamon-Raisin Rice Pudding

32-ounce carton vanilla-flavored lowfat yogurt
3 cups cooked white rice (cooked without salt)
$\frac{1}{2}$ cup raisins
$\frac{1}{2}$ cup water
1 teaspoon cinnamon (or to taste)

Day before: Drain yogurt (see instructions on page 13).

1. Combine raisins with $\frac{1}{2}$ cup water and cook over low heat until raisins are soft and plumped. Cool and drain well.

2. Place yogurt cheese in a medium-size bowl. Add rice, raisins, and cinnamon, stirring gently with a fork until well blended.

3. Spoon into individual serving dishes. Refrigerate until well chilled.

    Serves 8.

Per serving: Calories 178; Protein 6 gm; Carbohydrates 34 gm; Fat 2 gm; Cholesterol 3 mg; Calcium 136 mg; Sodium 43 mg

Rice and Fruit Cream

32-ounce carton vanilla-flavored lowfat yogurt
1 can (20 oz) pineapple chunks
2 cups cooked white rice (cooked without salt)

Day before: Drain yogurt (see instructions on page 13).

1. Drain pineapple and chop coarsely.

2. Combine yogurt cheese, pineapple, and rice. (Other cooked fruits, such as apples, pears, etc., may be substituted).

3. Pour into individual serving dishes and chill. Flavors blend after several hours.

    Serves 8.

Per serving: Calories 141; Protein 6 gm; Carbohydrates 25 gm; Fat 2 gm; Cholesterol 3 mg; Calcium 130 mg; Sodium 42 mg

Peach Rice Ring

32-ounce carton vanilla-flavored lowfat yogurt
2 tablespoons unflavored gelatin
$1/4$ cup water
$1/2$ cup water (or apricot juice)
1 jar ($4^1/2$ oz) strained peaches or apricots (baby food)
3 cups cooked white rice (cooked without salt)
Sliced peaches (optional)

Day before: Drain yogurt (see instructions on page 13).

1.   Soften gelatin in $1/4$ cup water for 5 minutes. Heat $1/2$ cup water (or juice) and add gelatin, stirring until gelatin is dissolved.

2.   Place yogurt cheese in a medium-size bowl, Gradually add gelatin mixture and peach puree, stirring gently with a fork or wire whisk until well blended. Stir in rice.

3.   Pour into a ring mold and chill for several hours or until firm. To serve, unmold and fill center with sliced peaches or other fruit, if desired.

Serves 8.

Per serving: Calories 167; Protein 8 gm; Carbohydrates 28 gm; Fat 2 gm; Cholesterol 3 mg; Calcium 129 mg; Sodium 46 mg

Apricot Mousse

32-ounce carton vanilla-flavored lowfat yogurt
2 cans (1 lb each) pitted apricots, packed in own juice
2 tablespoons unflavored gelatin

Day before: Drain yogurt (see instructions on page 13).

1. Drain apricots, reserving liquid. Soften gelatin in $1/4$ cup apricot liquid for 5 minutes. Place over low heat with remaining liquid and stir until gelatin is dissolved. Cool slightly. Puree apricots in blender or food processor.

2. Place yogurt cheese in a medium-size bowl. Gradually add gelatin mixture, stirring with a fork or wire whisk until well blended. Fold in apricots.

3. Pour into a large bowl or individual serving dishes. Chill several hours or until set.

    Serves 8.

Per serving: Calories 122; Protein 7 gm; Carbohydrates 20 gm; Fat 2 gm; Cholesterol 3 mg; Calcium 133 mg; Sodium 46 mg

Apple Mousse

32-ounce carton vanilla-flavored lowfat yogurt
$\frac{1}{2}$ cup frozen apple juice concentrate, thawed
1 tablespoon unflavored gelatin
$\frac{1}{4}$ cup confectioners' sugar
$\frac{1}{2}$ teaspoon cinnamon

Day before: Drain yogurt (see instructions on page 13).

1. Soften gelatin in apple juice for 5 minutes. Place over low heat and stir until gelatin is dissolved. Cool slightly.

2. Place yogurt cheese in a medium-size bowl. Gradually add apple juice mixture, sugar, and cinnamon, stirring gently with a fork or wire whisk until well blended.

3. Pour into a large bowl or individual serving dishes. Chill several hours or until set.

    Serves 6.

Per serving: Calories 148; Protein 7 gm; Carbohydrates 24 gm; Fat 2 gm; Cholesterol 4 mg; Calcium 168 mg; Sodium 57 mg

Minted Melon Parfait

32-ounce carton nonfat yogurt
2 ripe canteloupes
1 tablespoon unflavored gelatin
$^1/_3$ cup orange juice
$^1/_4$ cup confectioners' sugar (or to taste)
$^1/_2$ teaspoon mint extract (or 3 Tbsp creme de menthe)

Day before: Drain yogurt to make yogurt cheese (see p. 13).

1. Use melon baller to scoop out balls from canteloupes. Remove remaining fruit with a knife and puree in blender or food processor.

2. In a saucepan, soften gelatin in orange juice and canteloupe puree for 5 minutes. Place over low heat and stir until gelatin is dissolved. Cool slightly and add mint flavoring.

3. Place yogurt cheese in a medium-size bowl. Gradually add the gelatin mixture and sugar, stirring gently with a fork or wire whisk until well blended. Stir in melon balls.

4. Spoon into individual parfait glasses and chill until set.

    Serves 8.

Per serving: Calories 108; Protein 6 gm; Carbohydrates 20 gm; Fat <1 gm; Cholesterol 0 mg; Calcium 155 mg; Sodium 51 mg

Cantaloupe Fruit Delight

32-ounce carton nonfat yogurt
3 ripe cantaloupes
$1/4$ cup brown sugar
1 pound seedless green grapes
1 pint blueberries, picked over

Day before: Drain yogurt (see instructions on page 13).

1. Cut each cantaloupe in half and scoop out the seeds. Cut in half again. Chill.

2. Place yogurt cheese and brown sugar in a medium-size bowl, stirring with a fork or wire whisk until well blended. Fold in grapes and blueberries. Chill.

3. To serve, place a quarter-cantaloupe in a dessert dish and spoon some fruit mixture over it.

    Serves 12.

Per serving: Calories 128; Protein 5 gm; Carbohydrates 28 gm; Fat 1 gm; Cholesterol 0 mg; Calcium 118 mg; Sodium 42 mg

Swiss Cherries Romanoff

32-ounce carton nonfat yogurt
1 package (12 oz) frozen dark sweet cherries, thawed
1/4 cup cherry liqueur
2 tablespoons confectioners' sugar

Day before: Drain yogurt (see instructions on page 13).

1.   Drain the cherries. Combine cherries and liqueur, and set aside to allow flavors to blend.

2.   Place yogurt cheese in a medium-size bowl. Add cherry mixture and sugar, stirring gently with a fork until well blended.

3.   Pour into a large bowl or individual serving dishes. Chill several hours.

     Serves 8.

Per serving: Calories 92; Protein 5 gm; Carbohydrates 13 gm; Fat <1 gm; Cholesterol 0 mg; Calcium 150 mg; Sodium 41 mg

Creamy Fruit Pudding

32-ounce carton vanilla- or lemon-flavored lowfat yogurt
2 cups sliced strawberries
2 cups sliced peaches
$1/4$ cup brown sugar, or to taste

Day before: Drain yogurt (see instructions on page 13).

1. Place strawberries and peaches in separate bowls. Sprinkle fruit with sugar and mix gently. Set aside for about 10 minutes. Drain.

2. Spread a layer of strawberries on the bottom of a glass serving dish. Cover with a layer of peaches. Top with yogurt cheese. Chill and serve.

   Serves 8.

Per serving: Calories 118; Protein 5 gm; Carbohydrates 21 gm; Fat 2 gm; Cholesterol 3 mg; Calcium 134 mg; Sodium 43 mg

Lemon Bavarian Cream

32-ounce carton vanilla-flavored lowfat yogurt
$1/2$ cup lemon juice
1 tablespoon unflavored gelatin
$1/4$ cup confectioners' sugar
1 teaspoon grated lemon peel

Day before: Drain yogurt (see instructions on page 13).

1. Soften gelatin in lemon juice for 5 minutes. Place over low heat and stir until gelatin is dissolved. Cool slightly.

2. Place yogurt cheese in a medium-size bowl. Add the sugar and lemon peel, stirring gently with a fork or wire whisk. Gradually add gelatin mixture and continue stirring until well blended.

3. Pour into a large bowl or individual serving dishes. Chill several hours or until set.

   Serves 6.

Per serving: Calories 113; Protein 7 gm; Carbohydrates 16 gm; Fat 2 gm; Cholesterol 4 mg; Calcium 162 mg; Sodium 55 mg

Peaches in Sherry Cream

32-ounce carton nonfat yogurt
1/4 cup confectioners' sugar (or to taste)
3 tablespoons sherry
2 teaspoons vanilla, divided
4 large fresh peaches, peeled
2 cups orange juice

Day before: Drain yogurt (see instructions on page 13).

1. Place yogurt cheese in a medium-size bowl. Add sugar, sherry, and 1 teaspoon vanilla, stirring gently with a fork or wire whisk until well blended. Refrigerate.

2. Cut peaches in half and remove pits.

3. In a skillet, combine orange juice and 1 teaspoon vanilla. Add peaches in one layer. Bring to a simmer, cover pan, and simmer over medium heat until peaches are tender. Chill until serving.

4. To serve, place one peach half in a dessert dish and top with 1/4 cup sherry cream.

Serves 8.

Per serving: Calories 122; Protein 5 gm; Carbohydrates 23 gm; Fat <1 gm; Cholesterol 0 mg; Calcium 150 mg; Sodium 40 mg

Pineapple Fruit Boats

16-ounce carton vanilla-flavored lowfat yogurt
1 ripe pineapple with leaves
1 pint fresh strawberries, hulled and chopped
2 tablespoons brown sugar

Day before: Drain yogurt (see instructions on page 13).

1. Cut pineapple into quarters lengthwise. Remove flesh, keeping shell in one piece, including leaves. Chop fruit. Mix strawberries with sugar and set aside.

2. Place yogurt cheese in a medium-size bowl. Add pineapple and strawberries, stirring gently with a fork until well blended.

3. Spoon into pineapple shells and chill.

    Serves 4.

Per serving: Calories 159; Protein 5 gm; Carbohydrates 31 gm; Fat 2 gm; Cholesterol 3 mg; Calcium 143 mg; Sodium 44 mg

Ginger Cream Pineapple

16-ounce carton vanilla-flavored lowfat yogurt
1 can (20 oz) pineapple chunks, packed in own juice
1 tablespoon finely chopped candied ginger

Day before: Drain yogurt (see instructions on page 13).

1. Drain pineapple very well.

2. Place yogurt cheese in a medium-size bowl. Add ginger, stirring with a fork or wire whisk until well blended. Fold in pineapple.

3. Pour into a large bowl or individual serving dishes. Refrigerate until well chilled.

Serves 6.

Per serving: Calories 81; Protein 3 gm; Carbohydrates 15 gm; Fat 1 gm; Cholesterol 2 mg; Calcium 87 mg; Sodium 27 mg

Tropical Delight

16-ounce carton vanilla-flavored lowfat yogurt
1 can (20 oz) pineapple chunks, packed in own juice
2 tablespoons unflavored gelatin
1 pint fresh strawberries, hulled and chopped
2 tablespoons confectioners' sugar
1 medium banana, chopped

Day before: Drain yogurt (see instructions on page 13).

1.   Drain pineapple, reserving liquid. Soften gelatin in ¼ cup reserved liquid for 5 minutes. Add water to remaining pineapple liquid to equal 1 cup; add softened gelatin and stir over low heat until dissolved. Cool slightly.

2.   Mix strawberries with sugar and set aside.

3.   Place yogurt cheese in a medium-size bowl. Gradually add gelatin mixture and stir with a fork or wire whisk until well blended. Fold in pineapple, strawberries, and bananas.

4.   Pour into a large bowl or individual serving dishes. Chill several hours or until set.

Serves 8.

Per serving: Calories 116; Protein 4 gm; Carbohydrates 23 gm; Fat 1 gm; Cholesterol 1 mg; Calcium 76 mg; Sodium 24 mg

Strawberries Romanoff

32-ounce carton vanilla-flavored lowfat yogurt
1 quart fresh strawberries
1 tablespoon orange liqueur

Day before: Drain yogurt (see instructions on page 13).

1. Wash and hull strawberries and place in a large serving bowl.

2. Place yogurt cheese in a medium-size bowl. Add the liqueur, stirring gently with a fork or wire whisk until well blended. Pour over the strawberries and refrigerate at least 1 hour before serving.

    Serves 8.

Per serving: Calories 68; Protein 5 gm; Carbohydrates 9 gm; Fat <1 gm; Cholesterol 0 mg; Calcium 150 mg; Sodium 41 mg

Coeur a la Creme

32-ounce carton nonfat yogurt
1 teaspoon vanilla
¼ cup confectioners' sugar (or to taste)
2 cups fresh strawberries (or raspberries)

Day before: Drain yogurt (see instructions on page 13).

1.   Place yogurt cheese in a medium-size bowl. Add the vanilla and sugar, stirring gently with a fork or wire whisk until well blended.

2.   Line a heart-shaped mold with plastic wrap. Spoon yogurt cheese into mold and smooth the top. Refrigerate several hours or until well chilled. To serve, place plate over mold and invert. Remove wrap. Serve with fresh strawberries or raspberries.

   Serves 6.

Per serving: Calories 91; Protein 6 gm; Carbohydrates 15 gm; Fat <1 gm; Cholesterol 0 mg; Calcium 194 mg; Sodium 54 mg

Lemon Fruit Dip

16-ounce carton nonfat yogurt
3 tablespoons confectioners' sugar
1 teaspoon lemon juice (or to taste)
1 teaspoon grated lemon peel

Day before: Drain yogurt (see instructions on page 13).

1. Place yogurt cheese in a medium-size bowl. Add sugar, lemon juice, and grated lemon peel, stirring with a fork or wire whisk until well blended. Chill until serving time.

2. Serve in a small bowl placed in the center of a platter. Surround with fruit slices and strawberries for dipping.

    Makes 1 cup.

Per tablespoon: Calories 16; Protein 1 gm; Carbohydrates 3 gm; Fat 0 gm; Cholesterol 0 mg; Calcium 35 mg; Sodium 10 mg

Ginger Fruit Dip

16-ounce carton vanilla-flavored lowfat yogurt
1 medium banana, mashed
¼ teaspoon grated ginger root (or ⅛ tsp ground ginger)

Day before: Drain yogurt (see instructions on page 13).

1. Place yogurt cheese in a medium-size bowl. Add banana and ginger, stirring with a fork until well blended. Chill until serving.

2. Serve in a small bowl placed in the center of a platter. Surround with fruit slices and strawberries for dipping.

    Makes 1¼ cups.

Per tablespoon: Calories 19; Protein 1 gm; Carbohydrates 3 gm; Fat <1 gm; Cholesterol <1 mg; Calcium 24 mg; Sodium 8 mg

Chapter 5

Crepes, Cream Puffs & Bars

Chocolate Cream Puffs

Puff Pastry: $\frac{1}{2}$ cup water
2 tablespoons vegetable oil
$\frac{1}{2}$ cup flour
$\frac{1}{4}$ teaspoon salt
2 eggs

Filling: 32-ounce carton nonfat yogurt
$\frac{1}{4}$ cup confectioners' sugar
1 teaspoon vanilla
1 tablespoon unsweetened cocoa

Day before: Drain yogurt (see instructions on page 13).

1. Preheat oven to 450 degrees. Lightly grease a cookie sheet.

2. In a saucepan, heat water and oil to boiling. Beat in flour and salt all at once and stir vigorously until mixture leaves the sides of the pan and forms a ball. Remove from heat and beat in eggs, one at a time, until mixture is smooth. Spoon onto the cookie sheet in 8 mounds, leaving about 2 inches between them for spreading.

3. Bake for 10 minutes. Reduce heat to 400 degrees and continue baking for 15 to 20 minutes, until pastry is puffed and golden brown. Remove puffs to wire rack to cool.

4. Place yogurt cheese in a medium-size bowl. Add the sugar, vanilla, and cocoa, stirring gently with a fork or wire whisk until well blended. Chill.

5. Slice puffs in half and fill just before serving. Serves 8.

Per serving: Calories 135; Protein 7 gm; Carbohydrates 14 gm; Fat 5 gm; Cholesterol 68 mg; Calcium 149 mg; Sodium 126 mg

Strawberry Cream Puffs

32-ounce carton nonfat yogurt
10-ounce package frozen strawberries in syrup, thawed
Sugar to taste (optional)

Day before: Drain yogurt (see instructions on page 13).

1.   Place yogurt cheese in a medium-size bowl. Add strawberries, including the syrup. Stir gently with a fork until well blended.

2.   Make cream puffs as for Chocolate Cream Puffs (page 111). Fill with strawberry mixture just before serving, spooning any extra over the top.

     Serves 8.

Per recipe: Calories 143; Protein 7 gm; Carbohydrates 17 gm; Fat 5 gm; Cholesterol 68 mg; Calcium 153 mg; Sodium 196 mg

Pineapple Crepes

Crepes: 2 eggs
$1/2$ teaspoon sugar
1 cup water
1 cup flour

Filling: 16-ounce carton nonfat yogurt
$1/4$ cup confectioners' sugar
1 can (20 oz) pineapple chunks, packed in own juice
1 tablespoon kirsch (optional)

Day before: Drain yogurt (see instructions on page 13).

1. To make crepes, combine batter ingredients, mixing until well blended. Refrigerate for 1 hour. Grease a 7-inch fry pan lightly and place over medium heat until hot. Remove from heat and pour about 2 tablespoons of batter into the pan. Tip to spread batter thinly over the bottom. Return to heat and cook until top of crepe is dry and edges begin to brown. Loosen edges and drop the crepe onto a towel. Continue until all the batter is used. You should have 16 crepes.

2. Drain pineapple, reserving 2 tablespoons juice. Place yogurt cheese in a medium-size bowl. Add the sugar, kirsch and reserved pineapple juice, mixing gently with a fork or wire whisk until well blended. Chill.

3. To serve, spoon 2 tablespoons filling down the center of each crepe and roll. Place seam side down on a serving plate and top with pineapple chunks.

Serves 8 (2 crepes per serving).

Per serving: Calories 151; Protein 6 gm; Carbohydrates 28 gm; Fat 2 gm; Cholesterol 68 mg; Calcium 89 mg; Sodium 39 mg

Strawberry Crepes

Crepes: 2 eggs
$1/2$ teaspoon sugar
1 cup water
1 cup flour

Filling: 32-ounce carton nonfat yogurt
$1/4$ cup sugar confectioners' sugar
1 teaspoon lemon juice

Topping: 2 cups fresh strawberries, sliced

Day before: Drain yogurt (see instructions on page 13).

1. To make crepes, combine batter ingredients, mixing until well blended. Refrigerate for 1 hour. Grease a 7- inch fry pan lightly and place over medium heat until hot. Remove from heat and pour about 2 tablespoons of batter into the pan. Tip to spread batter thinly over the bottom. Return to heat and cook until top of crepe is dry and edges begin to brown. Loosen edges and drop the crepe onto a towel. Continue until all the batter is used up. You should have 16 crepes.

2. Place yogurt cheese in a medium-size bowl. Add the sugar and lemon juice, mixing gently with a fork or wire whisk until well blended. Spoon 2 tablespoons down the center of each crepe and roll. Place seam side down in a shallow baking pan and chill until serving time.

3. May be served chilled or hot. To serve hot, preheat oven to 400 degrees and heat crepes about 3 minutes. Spoon strawberries over crepes just before serving.

Serves 8 (2 crepes per serving).

Per serving: Calories 140; Protein 8 gm; Carbohydrates 22 gm; Fat 2 gm; Cholesterol 68 mg; Calcium 154 mg; Sodium 58 mg

Lisa's Strawberry Corn-Cake

32-ounce carton vanilla-flavored lowfat yogurt
$^3/_4$ cup yellow corn meal
5 $^1/_2$ cups cold water
2 tablespoons diet margarine
$^1/_2$ teaspoon salt
$^1/_2$ teaspoon sugar
1 pint fresh strawberries, sliced

Day before: Drain yogurt (see instructions on page 13).

1. In a saucepan, stir together corn meal and water. Bring to a simmer, stirring often. Add margarine, salt, and sugar and simmer for 35 to 40 minutes. Pour into an 8-inch square baking dish. Chill for several hours or until firm.

2. To serve, cut corn-cake into 2-inch squares, top with strawberries and yogurt cheese.

    Serves 16.

Per serving: Calories 67; Protein 3 gm; Carbohydrates 10 gm; Fat 2 gm; Cholesterol 2 mg; Calcium 64 mg; Sodium 106 mg

Dessert Kugel

32-ounce carton vanilla-flavored lowfat yogurt
1 1/2 matzo squares
1 cup apple juice
2 tablespoons cornstarch
2 eggs, lightly beaten (for substitutes, see page 16)
1 cup chopped apples
1/4 cup raisins
1 teaspoon cinnamon

Day before: Drain yogurt (see instructions on page 13).

1. Break whole matzos in half. Place in shallow dish and pour in apple juice. Let stand until juice is absorbed.

2. Place yogurt cheese in a medium-size bowl. Add the cornstarch, mixing gently with a fork or wire whisk until well blended. Stir in the eggs.

3. In a separate bowl, combine apples, raisins, and cinnamon.

4. With a spatula, place a soaked matzo piece in the bottom of a lightly greased casserole. Spread with one-third of the yogurt cheese and sprinkle with half the apple-raisin mixture. Repeat, ending with a layer of yogurt cheese. Smooth the top with a spatula. Refrigerate for 2 hours or longer.

5. Bake in a 325 degree oven for about 40 minutes. Serve warm or chilled. Serves 8.

Per serving: Calories 158; Protein 7 gm; Carbohydrates 25 gm; Fat 3 gm; Cholesterol 71 mg; Calcium 137 mg; Sodium 59 mg

Light Fruit Bars

16-ounce carton vanilla-flavored lowfat yogurt
2 tablespoons unflavored gelatin
$^1/_2$ cup orange juice
1 tablespoon lemon juice
3 egg whites
$^1/_4$ cup sugar

Day before: Drain yogurt (see instructions on page 13).

1. Preheat oven to 325 degrees.

2. Soften gelatin in orange juice for 5 minutes. Then heat and stir until gelatin is dissolved. Cool slightly.

3. Place yogurt cheese in a medium-size bowl. Gradually add gelatin mixture, stirring gently with a fork or wire whisk until well blended.

4. In a separate bowl, beat egg whites until foamy. Gradually add sugar and continue to beat until moist, soft peaks form when beater is withdrawn. Fold into yogurt cheese mixture.

5. Pour into an 8-inch square pan and bake 35 minutes. Cool and refrigerate. Cut into 2-inch squares.

    Serves 16.

Per serving: Calories 38; Protein 3 gm; Carbohydrates 6 gm; Fat <1 gm; Cholesterol 1 mg; Calcium 32 mg; Sodium 21 mg

117

Cherry Chocolate Brownie Bars

16-ounce carton vanilla-flavored lowfat yogurt
$^3/_4$ cup water, divided
2 tablespoons unflavored gelatin
5 tablespoons unsweetened cocoa
$^1/_2$ cup black cherry fruit spread
3 egg whites
$^1/_4$ cup sugar

Day before: Drain yogurt (see instructions on page 13).

1. Preheat oven to 325 degrees.

2. Soften gelatin in $^1/_4$ cup water for 5 minutes. Heat $^1/_2$ cup water and stir in cocoa and gelatin. Stir until dissolved. Cool slightly.

3. Place yogurt cheese in a medium-size bowl. Add cherry spread, stirring gently with a fork or wire whisk until well blended. Gradually blend in gelatin mixture.

4. In a separate bowl, beat egg whites until foamy. Gradually add sugar and continue to beat until moist, soft peaks form when beater is withdrawn. Fold into yogurt cheese mixture.

5. Pour into an 8-inch square pie pan and bake 30 minutes. Cool on a wire rack. Refrigerate until chilled. Serves 8.

Per serving: Calories 118; Protein 6 gm; Carbohydrates 23 gm; Fat 1 gm; Cholesterol 1 mg; Calcium 66 mg; Sodium 41 mg

Banana Clafouti

32-ounce carton vanilla-flavored yogurt
1 whole egg plus 2 egg whites, slightly beaten
1/2 cup lowfat milk
1/4 cup all purpose flour
1 tablespoon grated orange peel
2 tablespoons sugar
3 large ripe bananas

Day before: Drain yogurt (see instructions on page 13).

1. Preheat oven to 375 degrees.

2. In a medium-size bowl, combine the eggs, milk, flour, and grated peel, stirring with a wire whisk until well mixed. Add the yogurt cheese and stir gently to combine.

3. Lightly grease an 8-inch square baking dish and sprinkle the sugar on the bottom. Cut each banana into 3 lengthwise strips. Place bananas on the bottom of the pan and cover with yogurt mixture. Bake 40 to 50 minutes. Cool on a wire rack for 15 minutes and serve.

Serves 8.

Per serving: Calories 187; Protein 8 gm; Carbohydrates 33 gm; Fat 3 gm; Cholesterol 38 mg; Calcium 151 mg; Sodium 70 mg

Chapter 6

Crusts & Toppings

Pie Crust

Most of the recipes for cheesecakes and for pies do not include a crust. A crust can add 100 percent or more to the fat and calories of a pie. We have found that a crust is not necessary for a dessert to be satisfying or even for holding a slice together.

In place of a crust, you may wish to use a light crumb dusting in the pan. Lightly grease the pan and sprinkle with about one-half cup crumbs. Shake to distribute the crumbs on bottom and sides. Invert pan to remove excess crumbs.

There will be times that you will want to serve a pie or cheesecake that has a more "traditional" look. Or maybe you just want to splurge.

The following pie crusts will add about 50 calories or so to each serving. The nutritional analysis has been included for recipes that give specific ingredients and quantities.

Crumb Crust

¾ cups crumbs (about 9 graham cracker squares*
    or 9 zweiback slices)**
2 tablespoons softened diet margarine

1.   Mix ingredients and press into pie pan. Chill for 10 to
15 minutes before filling.

    *2 squares = 1 whole graham cracker.

    **Other kinds of crumbs that can be used include those
from cookies, crackers, dry cereals (cornflakes, etc), and
dry bread. Sugar may be added, if desired.

Peanut Butter Crust

9 zweiback slices
2 to 4 tablespoons peanut butter

1. Break up zweiback slices into small pieces, and place in a food processor or blender with the peanut butter. Process until well blended.

2. Press into a 9-inch pie pan and chill for 10 to 15 minutes before filling.

Meringue Shell

3 egg whites, room temperature
$1/2$ cup sugar (preferably superfine)

1. Preheat oven to 300 degrees. Lightly grease a 9-inch pie pan.

2. Beat egg whites until foamy. Gradually add sugar a tablespoon at a time, continuing to beat until moist, stiff peaks form when beater is withdrawn.

3. Spoon into pie pan, lightly smoothing to cover bottom and sides. Bake for 1 hour or until crisp and light brown. Cool on a wire rack to room temperature before filling.

    Serves 8.

Per serving: Calories 54; Protein 1 gm; Carbohydrates 13 gm; Fat 0 gm; Cholesterol 0 mg; Calcium 1 mg; Sodium 19 mg

Toppings

There are as many options for glazes and other toppings as there are cheesecake flavors. Fresh fruits, whole or sliced, add color and flavor to a cheesecake or pie. A light glaze over the fruit adds sparkle and a festive touch for a party dessert.

Although many of these toppings taste great on a cheesecake, some of the recipes can be used instead of a high-fat, high-calorie topping on other desserts. The pineapple topping, for example, can substitute for frosting on just about any kind of cake. The vanilla frosting, made with yogurt cheese (of course!) is the perfect low-fat, low-calorie replacement for a butter cream or cream cheese frosting on any cake.

When your dessert calls for whipped cream topping, our answer is vanilla yogurt cheese. You can use it plain, or you can add a liqueur or a flavoring such as cinnamon or vanilla. Spread the "whipped cream" over the pie or cake or serve in a separate bowl.

The nutritional analysis has been included for recipes that give specific ingredients and quantities.

Pineapple Topping

1 can (20 oz) crushed pineapple or pineapple tidbits
2 tablespoons cornstarch
1 tablespoon lemon juice (optional)

1. Drain pineapple, reserving juice. In a saucepan, mix the cornstarch with a small amount of the juice.

2. Add remaining juice and stir over medium heat until thickened and clear. Add pineapple and cook a few minutes longer. Cool slightly.

    Makes about 2 cups.

Cherry Glaze

¾ cup liquid from red sour cherries (16 oz can)
¼ cup sugar
1 tablespoon cornstarch

1. If there is not enough liquid from cherries, add water to make ¾ cup liquid.

2. Combine sugar and cornstarch in a saucepan. Slowly add liquid, stirring continuously with a wire whisk. Place on low heat and continue stirring until mixture has thickened and is clear. Cool slightly before using.

Makes about ¾ cup.

Fruit Glaze

1/2 cup apricot jam or raspberry jam*

1. Pour jam or fruit spread into a strainer placed over a saucepan, and force through with a wooden spoon.

2. Stir over low heat until melted. Cool slightly.

3. Spoon over the top and sides of a cheesecake. Or decorate cake with strawberry halves, kiwi slices, or other fresh fruit, and brush the glaze over the fruit.

    Makes 1/2 cup.

    *Raspberry fruit spread may be substituted.

Strawberry Sauce

1 quart strawberries, washed and hulled, or 12 oz package
    frozen strawberries, thawed and drained
Sugar to taste
1 tablespoon lemon juice

1. Place strawberries, sugar, and lemon juice in food
    processor and process until pureed and sugar is
    dissolved. May also be pureed with an electric mixer.

2. Pour over dessert just before serving.

    Makes about 2 cups (fresh) or 1½ cups (frozen).

Dessert Sauce

16-ounce carton nonfat yogurt
2 tablespoons sugar
$\frac{1}{2}$ teaspoon vanilla
1 tablespoon sweet liqueur (orange, cherry, vanilla, etc.)

Day before: Drain yogurt (see instructions on page 13).

1. Place yogurt cheese in a medium-size bowl. Add the sugar, vanilla, and liqueur, stirring gently with a fork or wire whisk until well blended.

2. Serve with strawberries, peaches, grapes, or other fresh fruit.

    Makes 1 cup.

Per ounce: Calories 38; Protein 2 gm; Carbohydrates 5 gm; Fat 0 gm; Cholesterol 0 mg; Calcium 70 mg; Sodium 20 mg

Orange Topping

1 cup orange juice
1 tablespoon sugar (optional)
2 tablespoons cornstarch
1 orange, peeled and sectioned

1. In a saucepan, mix the cornstarch with a small amount of juice. Add sugar and remaining juice and stir over medium heat until thickened. Cool slightly.

2. Spread half the mixture over a cake and decorate with orange sections dipped in remaining mixture.

    Makes topping for 1 cake or pie.

Entire recipe: Calories 280; Protein 3 gm; Carbohydrates 69 gm; Fat <1 gm; Cholesterol 0 mg; Calcium 76 mg; Sodium 0 mg

Creamy Vanilla Topping

8 ounce carton vanilla-flavored lowfat yogurt

1. Drain yogurt to desired consistency, about 2 hours.

2. Spread over any cheesecake or other dessert. For use on a baked cheesecake, remove the cheesecake from oven, allow to cool slightly (about 10 minutes), spread with topping and bake for 5 minutes.

    Makes topping for 1 cheesecake.

    For a sweeter topping, sugar and vanilla extract may be added to taste. The recipe can be varied by adding any desired fruit or flavoring.

Strawberry Cream

32-ounce carton nonfat yogurt
10-ounce package frozen strawberries, thawed
Sugar to taste (optional)

Drain yogurt for 1¹/₂ to 2 hours (to remove about 1 cup whey).

1. Place yogurt cheese in a medium-size bowl. Add straw-
    berries with the syrup. Stir gently with a fork until well
    blended.

2. Keep on hand as topping, light lunch, or dessert.

    Makes a big bowlful! (About one quart.)

    Variations are unlimited. Use other frozen fruit or
    cooked fresh fruit.

Vanilla Frosting

Use to frost any layer cake, to reduce the fat and calories.

16-ounce carton vanilla-flavored lowfat yogurt
$1/2$ cup confectioners' sugar
$1/2$ teaspoon vanilla

Day before: Drain yogurt (see instructions on page 13).

1. Place yogurt cheese in a medium-size bowl. Gradually add confectioners' sugar, stirring with a fork or wire whisk until well blended. Stir in vanilla. Refrigerate until chilled.

2. Spread on cake just before serving.

   Makes 1 cup (enough to frost one 9-inch square cake).

Per tablespoon: Calories 31; Protein 1 gm; Carbohydrates 6 gm; Fat 1 gm; Cholesterol 1 mg; Calcium 30 mg; Sodium 10 mg

Index

137

SHOPPING INFORMATION

Not Just Cheesecake: The Low-Fat, Low-Cholesterol, Low-Calorie Great Dessert Cookbook. 101 quick and easy recipes. $9.95

Really Creamy™ Yogurt Cheese Funnel. Engineer-designed with special micro-sized mesh lining. Makes yogurt cheese the easy way. Folds flat to store. $9.95

7-inch springform pan. Best size for cheesecake recipes in this book. Tin-plated steel $6.95, or heavy-duty aluminum (steel clasp) $12.95.*

ᴏᴏᴏ

BACK TROUBLE: A New Approach to Prevention and Recovery. Practical help for back, neck and shoulder pain, based on the Alexander Technique, a natural way to heal. 170 photos and illustrations. pb $9.95

MEMORY FITNESS OVER 40. For a better memory at any age. Minimize age-related memory loss. Cloth $14.95

STAND TALL! The Informed Woman's Guide to Preventing Osteoporosis. The first and still the best and most complete guide to understanding and prevention. Guidelines for exercise, nutrition, dietary supplements, and hormone replacement. Easy to understand. Cloth, $12.95

THE STRONG BONES DIET: The High-Calcium, Low-Calorie Way to Prevent Osteoporosis. Dietary approach to calcium without gaining weight. Includes recipes, menus, planting guide for high-calcium vegetables, and a calcium/calorie counter. Cloth $14.95

WOMEN TAKE CARE: The Consequences of Caregiving in Today's Society. Covers crucial issues that concern families of the chronically ill. Practical information about legal and financial matters, etc., plus caregivers own stories. Especially valuable for younger women in preparing for the future. Cloth $16.95, pb $9.95

ᴏᴏᴏ

The above items may be ordered from Triad Publishing Co., 1110 NW 8th Ave., Gainesville, FL 32601. Enclose payment plus shipping & handling: $2 first item, .50 each addl. item. Fla. residents add 6% tax.

* Subject to availability. All prices subject to change without notice.   (NJC:6/88)